America's Genius

America's Genius

Jonathan Edwards

Christian Timothy George

CF4•K

Copyright © Christian Timothy George 2008
Reprinted 2015
Paperback ISBN: 978-1-84550-329-1
Epub ISBN: 978-1-84550-901-9
Mobi ISBN: 978-1-84550-902-6

Christian Focus Publications,
Geanies House, Fearn, Tain, Ross-shire,
IV20 1TW, Scotland, U.K.
www.christianfocus.com;
email: info@christianfocus.com

Thinking Further Topics; Life Summary and Timeline
Copyright © 2008 Christian Focus Publications
Cover design by Daniel van Stratten
Cover illustration by Fred Apps

Printed and bound in Denmark by Nørhaven

All rights reserved. No part of this publication may be reproduced, stored in a retrieval system, or transmitted, in any form, by any means, electronic, mechanical, photocopying, recording or otherwise without the prior permission of the publisher or a licence permitting restricted copying. In the U.K. such licences are issued by the Copyright Licensing Agency, Saffron House, 6-10 Kirby Street, London, EC1 8TS. www.cla.co.uk

For Nic, Stephanie, and
Andrew Francis

Contents

Introduction 9
Sisters and Spiders 11
Swamp Prayers 21
Food Fight 31
Dock Discipline 47
Cured by Sickness 59
Judgment Day 71
Awakening 85
Last of the Mohicans 97
Transition Time 109
Living Again 123
Author's Note 135
Jonathan Edwards Timeline 136
Thinking Further Topics 138
Life Summary 147
Quotes of Jonathan Edwards 148
Sources and Bibliography 155

Introduction

Jonathan Edwards was a writer, preacher, and missionary who sparked spiritual awakening throughout the colonies of New England. In an age of scientific discovery, Edwards saw God's beauty displayed most perfectly through nature. His journals are filled with drawings of plants, animals, and spiders because he knew that each one of them reflected the creativity of its Creator.

Though Edwards never raised his voice behind the pulpit, God used his clear, forceful thinking to persuade thousands of people to give their lives to Christ. Intellectually, there were few people who could match his genius and by the time he turned thirteen years old he had already left to go to college. Throughout his life, Edwards echoed God's glory, both in his devotional and family life. Strict discipline and prayer governed his days, along with the great joy that comes from delighting in God's presence. It is no wonder that Benjamin B. Warfield said, "Jonathan Edwards, saint and metaphysician, revivalist and theologian, stands out as the one figure of real greatness in the intellectual life of colonial America."

Sisters and Spiders

East Windsor, Connecticut, 1711

Jonathan Edwards ran through the thick forest behind his house. Pine trees whizzed by his head as he jumped over logs that lined the trail. He was taller than other eight-year-olds, and ran faster too. It was difficult growing up with seven sisters, four older and three younger. They were always talking about girly things and never enjoyed outdoor games. He lived in a world of women and knew that if he couldn't outnumber them, he could certainly outrun them.

Jonathan turned his head to see if his sisters were still chasing him. Suddenly, his foot caught the edge of a root and he fell face first to the ground. With a loud THUD Jonathan slammed into the dirt. "That was close," he thought, looking at a large rock near his head. This wasn't the first time he had taken a fall like this. His sisters often made fun of him for being so clumsy and it didn't help being the skinniest boy in East Windsor.

Out of the corner of his eye Jonathan saw something move. His knee was bleeding but he bent down to examine a large black spider climbing up its web. He loved spiders. He loved everything about them. He loved the way they could suspend themselves in the air, the way they almost danced across the earth. He even liked the way they ate their prey—very organized and orderly. But this was the biggest spider he'd ever seen. Jonathan kept a piece of paper in his pocket for moments like these and he quickly sketched the spider's outline. He carefully recorded every detail of the experience so he could review his drawing at the end of the day. The web was wonderful—a spindle of silver shining in the sun—until, that is, Jonathan destroyed it with a pebble.

"Jonathan!" his sisters yelled in the distance. "Father's home!" Jonathan couldn't believe his ears. He ran back through the forest. His father, Reverend Timothy Edwards, had served as a chaplain for a colonial military expedition against Canada. For ten years, New England had been at war with France and ever since Jonathan could remember he had heard stories about how Native Americans sided with the French to conquer Connecticut. His family lived in a constant state of fear. His mother often prayed for Jonathan's uncle, John Williams, who was taken prisoner by twenty native American warriors. While in captivity, the natives murdered his wife and two children. "Their souls were quickly taken into the presence of God," Jonathan's mother reminded him.

Jonathan's father loved his family very much and wanted the best for them. Like most fathers of the day,

Jonathan Edwards

he was the head of the household. He made the rules and enforced them too. He was strict and demanded perfection, teaching his children the Bible, Latin, and Puritan history. "Knowing the past will prepare you for the future," he often told them. But he was also very forgiving and gentle. Once, Jonathan accidentally launched a rock through a window, shattering it into a thousand pieces. Instead of yelling at him, his father calmly explained why it was necessary to control one's actions and consider the significances of decisions before they are made.

Late at night, Jonathan and his father stayed up and talked about God by the fireplace. Jonathan was so proud of his father. In his younger years, Timothy attended Harvard University and became a great preacher of the gospel. No other preacher in the area had overseen more spiritual awakenings. Jonathan always asked his father endless questions about faith and his father always had an answer. Except for one.

"How long will you be at war?" Jonathan once asked his father.

"Son, there are some things that only God must know. This is one of them."

Jonathan's mother, Esther Stoddard Edwards, was amazing too. She was just as smart as her husband, and witty. She was the village schoolteacher and did not tolerate disrespect. Since the Edwards family lived in a large three-story house that had seven rooms, Jonathan's mother insisted on having school inside her own house. Jonathan got his height from his mother and also his passion for learning. Throughout her life, she was as healthy as a horse and eventually lived into her late nineties—an extremely long life in those days.

But the sound of neighing horses and carriage wheels brought Jonathan's mind back to the present.

"Father!" the children shouted, running to the buggy. Jonathan ran past his sisters to greet him. He looked different in his military uniform, but still had the same towering presence.

"I come bearing gifts," his father said with a grin. Jonathan loved the gifts his father gave him. They were always toys and gadgets. Once, Jonathan received a clock and he took it apart piece by piece to see how it worked. "Take my luggage, boy, and be careful not to drop it."

Jonathan's mother ran outside and embraced her husband. It had been two long months since he left for the war and she had no guarantee that he would come home alive. "I missed you so much!" she said. "The children and I prayed for you every night. Are you hungry? I'll have the servants prepare a meal."

Jonathan wanted to know everything about the war as the family sat down together at the large wooden dinner table. It was big enough to seat all the Edwards comfortably, even Jonathan's seven sisters —Elizabeth, Esther, Anne, Mary, Eunice, Abigail, and Jerusha.

Before too long the food was passed down the table, the corn, the potatoes, and the chicken, but Jonathan

Jonathan Edwards

could not take his eyes off his father's hand and the deep cut running from his thumb to his wrist. "How did you get that cut?" Jonathan asked.

"I'll tell you after the prayer," his father replied. As the Edwards family joined hands, everyone bowed their heads. Everyone, that is, except Jonathan, who stared at his father's wound. "Almighty God, maker of heaven and earth, we know that before time began you already existed. You are the One who holds the whole world in your hand and nothing happens outside your control. We pray tonight for the safety of our home and the peace of our village. Thank you for protecting us from the Evil One and we ask that this food may nourish our lives as our lives nourish your kingdom. In the name of Christ Jesus we pray. Amen."

Jonathan couldn't hold it in any more. "Tell us," he said, "did you . . . kill anyone?"

His father shook his head. "No, but I saw many men die. Good men—Christian men. Some died by the arrow, others by the spear. I even saw women and children murdered before my very eyes."

"Savages!" Jonathan's mother screamed.

"No, Esther," Timothy said. "We are all savages. Where would any of us be without the grace of God? The Mohicans are a very advanced people who have families and children just like we do. I believe God has a very special plan for them."

"What about your cut?" Jonathan interrupted.

"Ah, you don't want to know about this," his father said, holding up his hand. Jonathan's sisters shrieked when they saw the gash. They all begged for him to tell.

"It was a cold morning," his father reluctantly began, "so cold that I can still feel the chill against my flesh. At about five o'clock, I heard a man scream. Running out of my tent, I saw a group of Mohicans shooting arrows at our camp. Several officers fired muskets in their direction, but the Indians kept charging. I rushed back into my tent and got on my hands and knees to pray."

"What did the Indians look like?" Abigail asked.

"Some had shaved heads and were covered in red paint. Others looked very similar to us, with modern clothes and leather shoes."

"Then what?" Jonathan exclaimed, scowling at Abigail for interrupting.

Jonathan's father closed his eyes. "All of a sudden, something sharp flew through the air. It had colorful feathers and glistened in the light. Before I could even move out of the way, I felt a sharp pain in my right hand." Timothy reached from below the table and pulled out a leather bag. "Would you like to know what cut my hand?" he asked.

Jonathan and his sisters nodded. Their mother was intrigued too.

Timothy removed a large stick from the bag and placed it on the table. "It's called a Tomahawk. I brought it back for you, Jonathan. But you have to promise not to swing it at your friends."

Jonathan couldn't believe his ears. "I promise!" he replied, grabbing the weapon. It was heavier than he expected and shiny too. He ran his hand up the wooden stick to the sharp stone that was attached to the top with rope and feathers. He had never seen such an interesting thing.

"Have I ever told you that the Bible is like a Tomahawk?" his father asked. The children, who were admiring Jonathan's present, shook their heads. "Ah yes, the Word of God is a powerful weapon," he said, opening his Bible to Hebrews 4: 12. "Listen to this Scripture reading: 'For the word of God is living and active. Sharper than any double-edged sword, it penetrates even to dividing soul and spirit, joints and marrow.'"

"The Bible doesn't look very sharp to me," Mary said, taking one last bite of potato.

"It's not the shape of the Bible that's sharp, Mary. It's the message of the Bible. God communicates his will to us through this sacred book. He instructs us how we are to act and think. The only problem is that by nature we do not want to hear it. We rebel against God and seek after our own pleasures. But the Bible cuts through all that. It cuts through our pride and reminds us that God has sent Jesus Christ to save his people from their sins. By believing in him, we can be forgiven and taken to heaven."

It always amazed Jonathan how his father saw everything through spiritual lenses. Since their home stood along a road parallel to the Connecticut River, Jonathan and his father often walked by the water, thinking about the God who once calmed the Sea of Galilee and told the waters to behave. His father once said, "Never forget that your ancestors journeyed as pilgrims to this New World so they could worship God freely. And in the same way, you are on a pilgrimage to heaven. There is another life to come, a heaven that is your true home."

"How did you escape the attack?" Mary asked.

"By the skin of my teeth!" her father said. "A great storm arose and the wind and rain were so fierce that our army was able to retreat. We lost a lot of men that day, Mary, but so did the Mohicans. Since my hand was injured, they allowed me to come home from the war earlier than I expected."

"Thank the Lord for that," Esther said.

"And if there's one thing I've learned," he continued, "It's that war and violence are terrible things. Children, I pray that God will spare you from experiencing it as I have."

Jonathan knew a lot about violence. His grandmother lived an immoral life, his great-aunt killed her newborn baby, and his great-uncle was an ax-murderer. It was a dangerous time, yet in the midst of it, Jonathan felt the peace of God. He felt the invisible comfort that comes from depending on Jesus Christ. Jonathan thought back to the beginning of the day when he tripped in the woods and almost hit his head on a large rock. "God, you are protecting me for a special reason," he wrote in his diary that evening. "A reason that is far greater than my mind can understand."

After everyone had gone to sleep, Jonathan stayed awake to read his Bible by candlelight. He often did this, not because his parents told him to, but because he wanted to know more about the God his ancestors loved so much. Pulling out the picture of the spider he drew earlier that day, he admired the creature.

Jonathan cleared his throat and looked seriously at the spider, pretending to be a preacher like his father. "Such is the destiny of all who forget God; so perishes the hope of the godless. What he trusts in is fragile; what he relies on is a spider's web. Job 8: 13–14." Jonathan remembered how the small pebble destroyed the web. His parents often told him that worldly attachments are undependable and disappointing. He needed something thicker than a spider's spindle to lean against. He needed God to be the Lord of his life. That night, he invited Christ to be the web that he leaned against and vowed to live like a pilgrim in this world.

"I will travel lightly through life," he wrote in his diary, "following the footprints of God wherever they lead. For I know that he will walk beside me on the way."

Swamp Prayers

East Windsor, Connecticut, 1712

Jonathan slouched in his chair as the teacher asked the question, "Who wrote the famous book, *Grace Abounding to the Chief of Sinners?*" The students looked at each other to see if anyone knew the answer. Jonathan knew, but he didn't say anything. He always knew. His mind was a labyrinth of answers and he pulled them out of his head with ease.

"John Bunyan," he whispered. But Jonathan's mind wasn't fully on his lesson as he was thinking about the marshes near his house. Jonathan loved the swamp. He loved the way giant insects flew from tree to tree. He loved the smell of it—like the smell of an old book. Besides, the spiders were always bigger in the swamp. Last week, he constructed a prayer booth there where he could go and talk with God. Jonathan's friends sometimes went there too, but they were more interested in playing in it than praying in it.

"Who can tell me what John Bunyan's book is about?" the teacher asked.

"It's the autobiography of an English preacher who was thrown in jail for proclaiming the gospel,"

Jonathan exclaimed. Suddenly his mind was back in the classroom and his daydreams were left behind. Everyone was surprised by his answer. The teacher, who was also his mother, was proud of him. She had taught him the puritan classics, even the ones that some ministers didn't know. Esther knew that her son was talented. Jonathan was far more intellectual than his peers, not only in religion, but also in philosophy, history, and mathematics. He was a genius.

"That will be all for today," she said, dismissing the students from class. One by one they grabbed their books and exited the Edwards' house. Jonathan didn't have to go very far since he lived there, but instead of going to his room he grabbed his prayer journal and set out for the swamp.

Fat, blue insects buzzed by his head as he walked past the river. The mud was thick beneath his feet, but he didn't care. "Adam and Eve were originally created to live in a garden," he thought. "Not a house." He loved nature. He loved the way wind brushed the forest, like a broom sweeping the leaves. Clouds and rain puzzled him, not to mention snow and ice. He wanted to study every creature he could find, especially the red beetles that lived in bark and the giant lizards that slithered up trees. Sometimes he even caught yellow caterpillars and counted their feet, one by one. For him, the great outdoors was heaven on earth and he enjoyed being around fuzzy critters even more than family and friends.

Jonathan Edwards

The prayer booth had been difficult to construct. In his diary, he had sketched the blueprints for it, taking information and strategies from the latest articles on log cabin construction. His father often went to Boston and New York and brought him magazines of all kinds. His mind soaked up the information, regardless of the subject. If it contained truth, Jonathan wanted to investigate it.

For weeks he had chopped down trees and hammered planks together for the prayer booth. The booth had to be perfect to meet his strict requirements and anything short of perfection would not be tolerated. Jonathan enjoyed mixing mud, grass, and water together to slop between the logs for insulation. He fit the logs together like links, being careful to leave room for windows. He even carved a wooden cross and nailed it to the top of the hut. "This is the finest prayer booth in New England," he told himself. "And perhaps in all the world."

Jonathan opened the door to the prayer booth and closed it quickly behind him. It felt good to be out of the classroom. The room was chilly inside, yet strangely comfortable. Autumns were always cold in New England and in the winter, the swamp froze so much that it was dangerous to enter it alone. Jonathan preferred cold weather to hot. He remembered a sermon his father once preached in which he asked the congregation, "Can you bear to live half an hour in fire? If not how can you bear to live an eternity in hell?" Several people gave their lives to God that day and since that Sunday, Jonathan developed a distaste for hot weather.

"I feel as if God has poured himself into my life today," he wrote in his prayer journal. "He has splashed me with grace and showed me his glory." Kneeling down upon a small pew he had built at the front of the cabin, Jonathan began to pray. "Forgive me, Father, for fighting with Mary yesterday and for letting my pride surface. You know that's the biggest area of weakness for me and . . ."

SLAM! The door swung open. "Hurry, shut the door!" yelled a classmate.

"No, you shut it!" the other said.

Jonathan opened his eyes. "What are you two doing? Can't you see I'm praying in here?"

"There's a witch after us. She chased us through the swamp."

Jonathan stood up to look out the window.

"No!" they said, pulling him to the floor. "She'll see you! She's got evil, green eyes and one glance from her will put a curse on you forever. Remember what happened in Salem not too long ago?"

Jonathan remembered. His parents often told him about the women who were accused of witchcraft and sentenced to death. "They were casting spells on people," his father had said, "and worse than that, they were accused of being friends with the devil himself." Jonathan was suspicious about those stories. His scientific mind struggled to understand the superstitious laws of Salem. Yet he was only nine years old and could not dismiss the possibility of their truth.

"How far was she behind you?" Jonathan asked.

"Not far enough," his friend replied. "She wore a large black hat and carried a broomstick. I think she was flying."

"That's impossible," Jonathan said.

"Not for a witch," he said. "Wait … I think I hear her."

The three boys held their breath, huddling beneath the pew. They heard footsteps, one after the next, closer and closer. Jonathan tucked his legs behind him so the witch couldn't see him through the window. He felt protected inside his cabin, almost as if God had wrapped him in a cocoon. But he trembled beside his friends.

"We're doomed. It's all over for us," one of them said. Memories of their short childhoods raced through Jonathan's mind as the bright beams of sunlight glowed through the foggy window. Jonathan stole a peek.

"What did you see?" they whispered.

Jonathan's eyes were wide with fear. "A dark hat," he replied, paralyzed with fear. Something scratched against the latch of the door.

"God help us," yelled one of Jonathan's friends. "She's coming inside!"

They shut their eyes as the door cracked open.

"Please don't curse us!" the other friend shouted.

A wiry woman with a long broomstick walked into the cabin. "Boooo!" she yelled, waving her hands above her head. "Boooo!"

Jonathan opened his eyes. "God rebuke you!" he shouted, standing to his feet. "In the name of Jesus, God rebuke you!"

Suddenly, the witch collapsed on the ground... in laughter.

"Mary? Is that you?" Jonathan asked.

Mary erupted in laughter and could not control herself. "You should have seen your face," she giggled. "Did you actually think I was a witch?"

Jonathan's friends laughed even harder. "You really fell for that one, Jonathan," they said.

"What? You knew about this?" he asked them.

They nodded and ran with Mary out of the cabin. Jonathan burned with anger against them. "One of these days, I'm going to leave this town," he thought. "And I will never see these people again." Too mad to pray, Jonathan ran outside. "Sinner souls!" he yelled as he saw his sister and two friends run out of the swamp. "You're going to pay for this!"

Jonathan knew that he was a sinner too. He felt it in his bones. The first lesson of his New England Primer textbook read, "In Adam's fall, we sinned all," and Jonathan rarely needed to be reminded. He had a hot temper, a sharp tongue, and his father often disciplined him for showing it. For years, his parents prayed that

Jonathan Edwards

he would grow up to be a man of God and someone once predicted he would be a preacher. Jonathan didn't know about that, but he certainly felt an inner war within him. Part of him wanted to go tackle his friends for making fun of him, while the other part sought to forgive them. "God," he prayed, "replace my anger with kindness, for you are often angry with me but show me mercy instead of justice."

Being the son of a preacher had been hard. Everyone in the small town looked at Jonathan to see how he behaved. They studied his actions and attitudes, judging his conduct more strictly than the other boys. He often avoided being around people and preferred being alone in the woods. That's where he heard God's voice the loudest. No one could judge him there. He often looked at the trees when he was upset and their gentle swaying back and forth calmed him down. Jonathan saw Christ's power clearly through nature—every growing blade of grass reminded him that God cares about the little things, the insignificant things. "If God cares so much for grass that people walk on, how much more does he care for me?"

Jonathan sat down beneath the shade of a tree, comforted by his thoughts. This was his favorite tree and he often studied insects crawling beneath its branches. Light dodged and danced through leaves, causing shadows that flickered on his face. This is where Jonathan went to read. As far as boys go, Jonathan read everything a boy could read. A good book was better than a piece of gold for him and he devoured scientific pamphlets; anything that kept him up-to-date on contemporary thought. Jonathan pulled out a brand new pamphlet from his school bag: *Isaac Newton's Theory of Gravitation*.

Jonathan vigorously read the article: "While sitting under an apple tree, Isaac Newton, profound thinker and physicist, discovers the theory of gravity." After Jonathan finished the read, he picked up a stone and threw it as hard as he could. With scientific eyes, he watched the rock soar into the air and fall back down to earth. He threw another one, this time sketching the angle of its curve into his diary. "Gravity," he mused. "What an interesting idea."

There were many interesting ideas of the day. John Locke, the great English writer, dominated the literary scene; the German mathematician, Gottfried Wilhelm Leibniz, was busy discovering calculus; and Johannes Sebastian Bach was polishing his masterpieces. It did not matter how complex a subject was, Jonathan wanted to master it. When he wasn't studying for school, he began writing poetry and playing music. "Harmony," he once wrote in his diary, "lies in everything. From the musical notes of a song to the complicated numbers of an equation, God has created a logical and orderly earth."

Jonathan leaned hard against the tree. "If gravity exists outside of me," he thought out loud, "and it keeps me anchored to the earth, perhaps it exists

Jonathan Edwards

inside me, too." He pulled out his Bible and turned to Romans 3:12: "… there is no one who does good, not even one." Jonathan pondered the passage. "If there is no one who does good then there must be a common force inside of all people that keeps us from doing good—a gravity of sin." Jonathan had never thought of sin like this before, but he felt it to be true. Every time his friends made fun of him he felt this gravity. Every time he felt like staying in bed in the mornings instead of reading his Bible, he felt this gravity. He even felt it during church, pulling his thoughts away from Christ and focusing them on the things of the world. "The gravity of sin," he said.

As he explored this idea, a spider lowered itself from a branch near the tree. It was hanging from a single thread of web, being blown back and forth by the wind. "You are a fascinating creature, Mr. Spider," Jonathan remarked. "Perhaps you will help me understand the gravity of sin." Taking a twig from the ground, Jonathan played with the piece of web supporting the spider. Every few seconds, he stopped to make note of the experiment in his journal. "The web is very weak," Jonathan noted. "And it would take very little effort to sever the spider from the branch."

Jonathan remembered John Bunyan's book, *Grace Abounding to the Chief of Sinners*. It was a favorite, if not his very favorite. He thought about how honest Bunyan was as he wrote about his addictions to sin and his wanderings from God. "But how can Bunyan be the chief of sinners," Jonathan thought, "when surely I am the one who best holds that title?" Jonathan thought about all the times he disobeyed his parents and even lied to them. He thought about his selfishness and his proud heart. "I am the spider, hanging above the heat of hell, by a single piece of thread."

As Jonathan walked back through swamp, he stopped inside the prayer booth. "It must be your grace, oh God, that keeps us from falling," he prayed. "At any moment you could cut our cords, but instead you hold us when we have nothing else to hold on to. You are our web that protects us from wind and witches. You keep us safe when all seems wrong and wicked in this world. You redeemed us by becoming one of us. And for that, oh Christ, I give you praise."

Jonathan picked up the broomstick that Mary had brought to scare him and swept the dirt out of the cabin. His Puritan ancestors once wrote that cleanliness is next to godliness. With each stroke of the broom, he confessed the dirt in his life that was separating him from God. He held nothing back. No sin was too small. He poured his heart out to God until there was nothing left to say. When the room was spotless, Jonathan took a deep breath and walked home. Though he trudged through mud and roots, his soul felt cleaner than ever. And he greeted Mary with a big fat hug.

Food Fight

Wethersfield Collegiate School Cafeteria, Connecticut, 1721

"Ouch!" Jonathan yelled as a potato smacked him in the head. He was seventeen years old and knew that this kind of behavior was unacceptable. Ducking for cover, Jonathan saw broccoli and squash whiz through the air. Chicken soup and fruit juice splashed against windows. The whole cafeteria was a war zone and all the students were involved. Jonathan, who was the school butler, hid beneath the carving table as his friends smeared cherry cobbler into each other's hair.

"You're acting like animals," Jonathan told them. "I shall have nothing more to do with you."

"You never have any fun!" Elisha Mix said, throwing a cucumber at him.

"I came to college to train my mind," Jonathan replied, scooping pieces of corn from his arm, "not my food throwing skills."

Elisha was Jonathan's roommate for the year and every night he went out to play while Jonathan read his books. Jonathan's mastery of languages allowed him to start college at the age of thirteen, several years before most boys. The average age for enrollment was sixteen and Elisha was jealous that Jonathan was smart enough to start so young. One day Jonathan wrote to his father: "Through the goodness of God, I am perfectly free of Elisha's janglings. Though he is training, like me, for the ministry, he acts half his age. The more time I spend with him, the more I want to spend with someone else."

The two boys were not best of friends by any means but both had to put up with each other.

Jonathan was now finishing his Master's level work. He wanted to know more about God and nature. There was no end to his brilliant thoughts. Though most of his friends were older, they acted younger and were annoyed with Jonathan for always having his nose in books.

"What's going on in here?" a teacher demanded, walking into the cafeteria. Just then Elisha launched a turkey leg into the air, hitting the teacher in the face. Silence settled over the whole room as Elisha realized what he had done.

"Who threw that?" the teacher asked. No one spoke up. Jonathan saw what his roommate had done and pointed his finger at him. Elisha scowled.

"Did you throw this, young man?" the teacher asked.

Elisha hesitantly nodded. "I'll get you back for this, Jonathan," he growled as the teacher grabbed his ear and dragged him down the hallway.

Jonathan Edwards

"I am only seventeen," Jonathan wrote in his diary that afternoon, "but I have no time to waste my life. There are too many things to learn, too many adventures to live. Time is a very precious thing and God is calling me to live it fully."

As Jonathan flipped through the pages of his diary, he remembered his senior year of college and how he grew deathly ill from a disease called pleurisy. For three weeks his lungs were so hot that they could barely hold their air. His throat burned with infection, his head swirled with fever, and he fell asleep, almost for the last time. "I confronted death face to face," his entry read, "and when I woke up the next morning I vowed to live each day as though it were my last."

"Why did you tell on me?" Elisha asked the following day.

"Because you were guilty," Jonathan replied without looking up.

Elisha grabbed the book Jonathan was reading and threw it against the wall.

"But I thought you were my friend!"

"I am your friend, but sometimes friends have to make the right decisions."

Elisha turned his back to Jonathan and picked the book off the ground. "I know you like to be alone in the evenings to read, but I want you to come with us tonight. I promise we won't play cards or break windows. There's someone I want you to meet. His name is Percival and I think you should tell him about how to become a Christian."

Elisha handed the book back to Jonathan. "Is he a student here at Wethersfield?" Jonathan asked.

"No, he lives about an hour's walk from here and insisted on meeting you. I told him that you were more knowledgeable about God than anyone I'd ever met so I promised to bring you to his house tonight."

Jonathan looked skeptical. "Is this a trick? Since when have you been interested in spiritual matters?"

"He really wants to meet you," Elisha replied. "He wasn't smart enough to come to college, but I think you would have a lot in common with him."

"I have so much work to do here," Jonathan said. "I'm busy writing a treatise called *Natural Philosophy*, but if he is really interested in knowing Jesus, I will come with you tonight."

"Great," Elisha said with a smile. "We will meet you by the library at 8:00 p.m. Don't be late." Elisha grabbed his coat and left the room.

Jonathan had a passion for people who wanted to know about the gospel. As a preacher's son, he saw how his father led people to the Lord and continued to spiritually feed them with his weekly sermons. There were nights when members of the congregation would weep and mourn over their sins in the family room of his house. Some would even stay all night, praying that God would show kindness and mercy on them. Jonathan saw it all. He saw the way God worked in his

Jonathan Edwards

small village, and deep down he wanted to be like his father. He seized every opportunity to tell his friends about Christ and since God was doing amazing things in Connecticut, many people were responding to the message of salvation. "I am going to meet a young man named Percival this evening," Jonathan wrote in his diary. "May the God who prepares hearts for himself, plough Percival's soul to receive the Savior."

Horses galloped by as Jonathan sneaked down the street. The moon was full that night, fuller than he had ever seen it. Since it was against school policy to leave the campus without permission, Jonathan walked slowly, hiding in the shadows. He knew that getting caught could mean serious punishment, perhaps expulsion. Yet, Percival needed to know about Jesus and he was willing to bear the consequences of his actions.

"Psss, down here!"

Jonathan saw Elisha hiding beneath a bush and ran over to him.

"Did anyone see you?" Elisha asked.

"No, I don't think so."

"Good. Once we get off of campus, we won't have to be so careful. Jonathan, I want to introduce you to my friends. This is William, George, Jacob, and Joshua."

Jonathan shook their hands. "It's a pleasure," he said.

"No, the pleasure is all ours," Jacob responded, grinning to the others.

"What's that in your hand?" George asked.

Jonathan held the book into the light. "It's my Bible. How can I share the gospel with someone without it?"

Elisha stepped in front of Jonathan. "Remember what I said? Jonathan is going to tell Percival about Jesus tonight."

Then Joshua looked confused. "But you said that…"

"That's right, Joshua," Elisha interrupted, "now we need to get going so we won't be late. Percival is counting on us."

One by one, the group of guys walked beside the wall of the library, pausing at every bush so no one would see them.

"Get down!" Elisha whispered. Several students passed by, talking about the girls they met on the other side of town.

"Her name is Rebecca," one of them said, "and she's very beautiful. She has long blonde hair and she's extremely smart."

As their voices dissolved into the distance, Elisha led his friends into the woods. Jonathan held his Bible closely at his side. He knew about the dangers of walking through the forest at night. Thieves and murderers lived here, not to mention snakes and other creatures that feed when the sun goes down. As a young boy, Jonathan was afraid of the dark. He heard stories of ghosts and wicked spirits that roamed the midnight woods. However, he would stay up late and read about how Jesus cast out demons and once he even drove

Jonathan Edwards

them into a herd of pigs. "God, keep me safe as we journey to see Percival," he prayed.

Looking behind him, Jonathan saw the lights of the campus slowly fade away. The thick forest was hard to walk through and his friends weren't making much progress.

"I think the road is coming up," Elisha said, holding back branches so his friends could pass through.

"Are you sure we are going in the right direction," George asked.

Elisha punched him in the arm. "Of course I'm sure. See, there's the path that leads to the road."

Jonathan unwrapped a thorny vine that had attached itself to his leg. Being taller than the others, and lankier, too, he always got tangled in plants and tripped over roots. His father once said, "Jonathan, you will be taller than most of your friends, but never forget that your perspective on the world will be higher too." Jonathan took his father's words seriously and tried to maintain a higher perspective on life. He tried to see God as greater and more powerful than most people imagined, but sometimes it was difficult, especially in the woods.

Jonathan was horrified as William inserted a fingerful of tobacco into a pipe and started to puff. "What are you doing?" Jonathan asked.

"It's called smoking," William replied. "And the whole world is doing it."

Jonathan had never seen anyone actually smoke before. His parents strictly forbade it because they believed it ruined a person's witness and led them to commit other sins of the flesh like dancing and drinking. "If only my father could see me now," Jonathan mused. "Here I am, running away from school, sneaking through the woods with friends who smoke."

"Would you like to try it, Jonathan?" Joshua asked, passing him the pipe.

"Absolutely not!" he said. "Bad company corrupts good character."

"Where did you hear that?" George asked.

Jonathan opened his Bible and said, "I Corinthians 15:33."

Jacob laughed. "And good character corrupts fun adventures."

"That's enough!" Elisha said. "If Jonathan doesn't want to have fun, we don't need to force him to."

As Jonathan walked behind the group, his thoughts turned upward. He examined the moon—the way it reflected the sun's brilliant rays. He looked at the stars twinkling against the velvet sky. "God, your work is truly amazing," he whispered. "You have ordained a plan for everything you have created. You tell the moon to spin around the earth and it obeys. You tell the clouds to hover through the sky and they obey too. Even the distant stars are not distant to you, for you are everywhere. You are so much bigger than I thought you were."

As a child, Jonathan grew up thinking that the world revolved around him. "I thought that I was the center of the universe," he once wrote in his diary. "And life existed to make me happy. But as I learn about God and his glory, I have come to the conclusion that the world revolves not around me, or anyone I know, but around God, and God alone. Everything exists for him, for his passion and his pleasure."

One day Jonathan read about a man named Nicolas Copernicus who discovered that the world revolved around the sun, not the other way around. After reading that article, Jonathan's view of life changed. He saw the world and everything in it through different lenses. No longer did life exist to serve his needs, but instead, he existed to serve the God who created him. It was a spiritual revolution in his life, a moment of transition and enlightenment, and Jonathan thought about that discovery as he looked up into the night. "If these trees can spread their branches to praise you," he prayed, "then I can too. Even if I am surrounded by a bunch of wicked boys."

Jonathan's friends were exchanging vulgar stories, but he was worshipping God behind them. Everything he saw reminded him of God's goodness. The rocks were not rocks to him, but rather, they were age-old witnesses to what God had accomplished in this New World. The breeze was more than a breeze to him. It was a symbol of the Holy Spirit that refreshed God's people and pushes them in the right direction. Life itself was becoming a journey to Heaven, and step after step, Jonathan was getting closer.

After an hour of walking, houses began to appear on the side of the road. "Are we there yet?" Jacob asked.

"Yes, I can see the house now," Elisha answered, pointing down the street. Its tall, plain chimney jutted into the sky, releasing puffs of smoke. Jonathan often sketched houses like these in his journals, but they appeared too ordinary for him. He preferred drawing what God had made—bugs and leaves—instead of what humans had made—barns and farms.

"Now keep your voices down," Elisha reminded. "We don't want to scare anyone before we see Percival."

Jonathan was ready to share the gospel. Dozens of Bible verses paraded through his mind. He was ready to talk about sin and grace and how God sent his son into the world to satisfy God's righteous wrath. "This is it," Jonathan said. "At last, I will share the hope that I have come to love."

A light rain began to fall as they ran past the front of the house. Jonathan pulled on Elisha's sleeve. "Why aren't we going to the front door?"

"Percival told me to come around to the back of the house. It's quieter back there and we can talk without disturbing his family."

This sounded odd to Jonathan, but he followed his friends around to the other side. They passed the chicken cage and the barn that held the horse's hay. They jumped over the fence that separated the tomatoes from the carrots. In the distance they could even see the glow of the moon shining off a nearby pond. When they arrived at the back door, Joshua, William, George, and Jacob stepped aside as Elisha led Jonathan to a pigpen.

Elisha pointed to a pig. "Jonathan, I would like to introduce you to Percival. He's not the best listener, but you can try to talk to him anyway." The pig looked up at Jonathan and began snorting and rolling in the dirt.

Everyone laughed, but Jonathan could not believe his ears. He had been tricked by Elisha in the meanest, most terrible way. How could he ever forgive him? Suddenly, the back door swung open and a man appeared. "What are you boys doing out here?" he asked.

William grabbed a rock and threw it at a window. Glass shattered and the man at the door grabbed a shovel and pursued the boys on foot. As they were running out of the yard, George grabbed one of the chickens and placed it in his pack. Jacob stole several tomatoes and put them in his pockets.

"How could you do this to me?" Jonathan asked, running as fast as his legs could carry him.

"I told you I'd get you back," Elisha said.

The group of boys darted down the road. Thunderclouds erupted and blinding lightning streaked the sky. The chicken was squawking loudly and George released it in the woods. Jonathan could barely see the road because the rain was so heavy, but he continued back the way they had come. This was the first time in his life that he enjoyed being tall enough to run faster than his friends.

Jonathan prayed that he would get back safely. "I never should have left my room tonight," he blurted. "What if someone finds out? What if my father hears of this? What if …"

"No more 'what ifs'" Elisha said calling out from behind him. "No one will know. We come out here every night and we've never been caught." Suddenly, Elisha slipped and fell on the ground. "Help!" he screamed as his friends continued to run through the woods. "Someone help!" Jacob pretended not to hear, along with the other guys and kept running.

But Jonathan heard. Turning around, he ran back to Elisha and picked him up.

"I can't go on," he said. "My ankle—I think it's broken."

Jonathan examined his leg. Elisha's ankle was twisted and starting to swell. Jonathan screamed for the other friends to come back but they were too far in the distance to hear. "I'm going to have to carry you," he said.

Elisha shook his head. "No, not after the way I treated you. Just leave me."

The rain was so fierce that Jonathan could barely hear, but he wrapped Elisha's arm around his neck and stood up. "You're coming with me," Jonathan yelled. Together, they limped through the forest, the dense shrubs and thorny vines, over the roots that reached up to grab their ankles, until they came to the edge of the campus. Elisha was heavy, but Jonathan was determined to take him safely home.

As they journeyed, Jonathan felt a peace settle over him. He was no longer angry with Elisha for tricking him and the feelings of hatred for the other boys were also gone. Huge raindrops fell into his eyes as he looked up at the ominous sky anyway. Black clouds swirled above, threatening and taunting him, but he felt an inward sense of God's love. He felt a soothing assurance that God was watching over him, protecting him from danger. And deep down, he knew that Christ had put him on this earth to help people find a way to their heavenly home.

Jonathan and Elisha snuck around the library where they had met earlier in the evening and trampled through the wet grass that led to their dormitory. Their friends had long since vanished and Jonathan stumbled into the room, out of breath, but out of the rain and thunder.

"Why did you help me?" Elisha asked, taking off his shoe to examine his ankle.

Jonathan didn't reply. He went into his room and grabbed a book off his shelf. There were many books in his room. He had books on plant life, physics, and chemistry, not to mention geography and map making. Grabbing a book of medicine, he returned to Elisha. "This book will help your ankle," he said. After reading several paragraphs, Jonathan tied his ankle up in a towel and elevated it on a wooden stool. "That should stop most of the swelling," he said. "At least until morning."

Elisha was grateful. "But you never answered my question. Why did you help me?"

"I helped you because that's what Jesus would have done. In fact, it's what he has done. Christ came to earth and limped beside us, agonized with us, and ultimately healed us from our sins. If Christ bent down and washed the dirt from his disciple's feet, as the Bible says, then how could I not help your ankle?"

Elisha thought about Jonathan's logic. "That makes sense," he said. "You always make sense. Please forgive me for tricking you. I knew that if I lied to you about Percival you would come with us. Turns out, it was me who needed to hear a word from God, not the pig. And you showed me Jesus in a way that no one ever has."

"I forgive you," Jonathan replied. "And by the way, Percival is a really good name for a pig."

Elisha laughed, "I'll tell the farmer that next time I see him!"

Jonathan laughed too as he rang the water out of his clothes.

Later on as Elisha snored in the corner Jonathan opened his diary and wrote, "God, thank you for showing me how to forgive Elisha not just with my lips, but also with my actions. Thank you for sending Jesus to hurt with us, limp beside us, and die for us on the cross. I will continue to lift you up every day, for you are highly exalted and powerful. Your glory has become the object of my eyes and I will forever praise your name."

Closing his eyes, Jonathan prayed a Puritan prayer his mother once taught him: "Lord, if my soul this night away you take, let me by morning in Heaven awake. Amen." It had been a rough day, but also a glorious one. And Jonathan couldn't wait to see what God would show him tomorrow.

Dock Discipline

Manhattan Island, New York City, 1723

Wooden cargo ships creaked and swayed in the waves of the Hudson River. Their sails rocked back and forth as the wind blew them beside the shore. Jonathan bent over to look at his reflection in the water. His dark brown hair hung below his ears and made his long face look even longer. It was not a normal haircut for nineteen-year-olds, but then again, Jonathan didn't feel normal.

"What's the matter?" John Smith asked.

"Nothing, really," Jonathan replied. "I think I'm just nervous about tomorrow."

John could see that there was something more on his mind. "I've known you for five months now. Ever since you came to live with us I've been praying for your sermons. God will bless your words tomorrow as he always does. But something else is wrong. You look paler than I've ever seen you. Have you even eaten today?"

Jonathan shook his head. "I can't eat. Not today."

"Why not?"

"God has convicted me of further sins," Jonathan said, "including gluttony. I've been experimenting with food to see just how much my body needs in order to survive. If I eat too much food, my senses grow dull and sinful passions rouse inside me."

John looked confused. "But you barely eat anything. You are skinny as the masts of those ships."

Jonathan looked out at the water. "There's another sin, too—vain-thinking. I've never been to a place like New York before, a sin city with ten thousand inhabitants. There's so much wickedness and immorality here and I fear it is beginning to rub off on me."

John threw a rock in the river. It skipped several times before plopping to the bottom. "No one's perfect," he said.

"I'm not trying to be perfect," Jonathan lied. "But I want to be as close to it as humanly possible."

Jonathan enjoyed talking with John. John's family had emigrated from England and the two always exchanged fascinating stories. Unlike his friends in college John would talk at length about God and about what he was doing in other parts of the world as well as in America. "Revival is brewing in our land," John would say. "Very soon, we shall see a spiritual awakening splash across the country." This excited Jonathan, who also observed this phenomenon.

As they walked, Jonathan passed an African slave market. "Ten years ago, nineteen African slaves were brutally murdered here for participating in an insurrection."

Jonathan Edwards

John glanced at the Africans who were being sold. "I believe God will judge our land for the way we have treated the Africans," he said. "If someone kidnapped me from my country, put me on a long boat ride to another land and forced me to work in their fields, I believe I would participate in an insurrection, too."

Jonathan nodded. "The Jewish population is not treated well here either. In fact, I was looking out the window yesterday and noticed that our Jewish neighbor was praying more fervently than I have ever prayed in my whole life. He took his faith more seriously than I have taken mine, and his devotion to God humbled me."

"Is that why you are experimenting with different forms of discipline?" John asked.

"Yes. New York is a cosmopolitan city and if I neglect disciplining myself here, I will be swept away with every passing pleasure."

"It still amazes me," John said, "that during your Master's Degree you were invited to be the supply preacher for the Presbyterian Church on Williams Street by the docks. How did you know it was God's will to come here?"

Jonathan stopped walking and pointed at the passing ship. "You see those sails?" he asked. "By themselves, those sails cannot move a ship. But when the captain orders his crew to raise them, the wind guides the ship in the right direction. I've never wondered about how to find God's will for my life. As long as my sails are up and I am listening to his voice, he always sends the wind. After graduation, God led me here to this church and I have never looked back."

"As you know, our church can be difficult to pastor at times," John said. "We were originally located at Wall Street and Broadway, but we split off from that church and started our own here by the docks. There are often conflicts between the Scots-Irish and the English members of the congregation. There are even rumors that if our church survives, they will call you to be the senior pastor. Would you be interested in taking that position?"

Jonathan thought about the opportunity. "Ever since I was a child, I've sensed that God was forming me to be the pastor of a church. He gave me a father who was a pastor and showed me how to preach the gospel."

"And your immense knowledge of the world would help you pull illustrations into your sermons that people would resonate with," John said. "I think you would make a fine pastor. You've certainly been a fine friend."

As they were walking, a girl approached them. "Excuse me," she said. "Can you tell me how to get to Wall Street?"

Jonathan tried not to stare, but he was mesmerized by her beauty. Dark flowing curls hung down her shoulders and her eyes sparkled like the sea he was standing beside. "I think it's that way," he said, pointing into the distance.

Jonathan Edwards

"What my friend means," John asserted, "is that if you take a right on the next street, go three blocks and turn left, you'll run right into it."

"Thank you," she said, continuing down the street.

Jonathan shook his head admonishing himself as the young woman walked away. It seemed that there was temptation everywhere – it was just so difficult sometimes to fight it. "I've decided to make a list of all the sins I am prone to commit and match each one with a discipline to get rid of it," Jonathan said. "For example, if I notice that I am being lazy and sluggish, I will discipline myself to read my Bible for two hours every morning until my laziness goes away. Or, in this case, if I am tempted to look at a girl and think impure thoughts, I will discipline my eyes to avoid staring at them. My parents told me about how Puritans disciplined their bodies in their quest for holiness. Some of them would spend a week fasting and praying. Others would memorize entire books of the Bible and repeat them over and over in their heads. I sense that my body craves discipline and my soul needs it for survival."

John had never met anyone so in tune with God. Every time they talked, Jonathan's insights startled him. "God is raising you up for something great," he said. "I don't know what God has in store, but he will bless all the energy you are using in your quest for godliness."

As they were talking, a group of ladies passed by. Jonathan was eager to begin his newly discovered discipline and he greeted them properly and then diverted his eyes. "See, that wasn't so bad," he told John just before catching his foot on the curb and falling to the ground.

John tried to catch his friend, but it was too late. "Maybe you should discipline your feet as well as your eyes," he said, laughingly.

The next morning, Jonathan woke up earlier than usual and opened his Bible to Proverbs 15: 32, "He who ignores discipline despises himself, but whoever heeds correction gains understanding." It was Sunday and Jonathan was nervous. Every time he preached he became nervous, not because he thought his sermons were useless, but because of all the people watching him. Groups of people made him uncomfortable and sometimes when he was proclaiming the gospel from the pulpit, he wished he were in the forest looking at nature and examining God's great creation.

"Here's your breakfast," Madam Susanna Smith said, opening the door to his room. She laid a tray of milk and boiling oats on his bed. "How did you sleep?"

"I tossed all night," Jonathan replied. "Sleep always evades me before I preach. But I must say, Madam, you and John have been most hospitable to me."

"It's our honor," she said. "Besides, hosting a preacher has been a privilege for us. And I know John has enjoyed talking with you. What is the topic of your sermon this morning?"

Jonathan Edwards

Jonathan grabbed his stack of handwritten notes. He never preached a sermon without notes; they were crucial to keep his thoughts organized. Every word had to be completely written out and memorized. He also never raised his voice in the pulpit because he believed that if God indeed gave him a word for the congregation, he should deliver that word calmly and with great respect. "Tomorrow, the title of my sermon is 'A Humble Attempt to Promote Discipline in the Life of a Christian and the Consequences of Tolerating Laziness.'"

Susanna was expecting a shorter title, but she smiled. "I am confident that God will open our hearts and heads to receive it."

Since the Smiths lived near the church, it only took about ten minutes to walk there. The church was plain and white, typical of Presbyterian churches of the day. Only in Catholic churches would art be tolerated inside the sanctuary, but Jonathan's parents did not allow him to see them. "Our Puritan ancestors broke away from that style of worship," his mother once said. "We believe that we cannot work our way to heaven. No matter how good we are, how smart we are, and how much we pray, we believe the Bible says that grace cannot be earned. Instead, it is a gift from God."

Jonathan liked gifts, though he rarely received any. He liked them for two reasons. First, they were free and unexpected. And secondly, they reminded him that life itself was a gift. It was a gift to be treated well, disciplined, and trained for service in God's kingdom.

As the Smiths walked into the church, Jonathan turned to John. "Something is not right," he said. "I cannot preach today."

"Why not?" John asked.

Jonathan didn't reply, but held the Bible tightly to his side, so tightly that his hands turned white.

"Jonathan, you're shaking," John said. "What's the matter?"

Other members of the congregation noticed Jonathan's uneasiness and began to whisper to themselves.

"I cannot preach today because I am not right with God," Jonathan said.

"Is there a problem here?" James Anderson asked, placing his hand on Jonathan's shoulder.

"No pastor," John said. "Jonathan is just feeling the heaviness of the preaching task."

"Ah", he replied. "Many preachers get the jitters before they step up to the pulpit. Preaching is a very serious matter and should not be taken lightly. Whenever a man claims to have a word from God, he best be sure it is from God. A very wise preacher once told me that God has put his word in my mouth, and I should be careful not to put my words in his mouth."

Jonathan nodded and thanked him for his counsel. "The Lord has not brought me this far," he said, "only to abandon me when I need him." After a short hymn

Jonathan Edwards

and a prayer for the sick, Jonathan stood up and walked to the pulpit. It was a massive pulpit placed near the center of the sanctuary. Jonathan grabbed the handrails and walked up the four steps leading to the top. Each step brought him closer to the moment when he would look out at the congregation.

There were only thirty people sitting in the pews, but they looked like a thousand. Jonathan was the youngest preacher they had ever seen. As he reached the top of the pulpit, he felt the burden of being the morning preacher. Each person in the congregation looked up to him, examined him, and waited to hear something special. "Well," Jonathan thought, "here we go."

After reading the Scripture passage and the title of his sermon, Jonathan cleared his throat and began to speak. "Two hundred years ago, God convicted his church to start a reformation." Jonathan's voice wavered, but he continued. "God raised up men like Martin Luther and John Calvin and together they brought revival to the hearts and souls of people who had been ensnared by wicked doctrines. This morning, we shall examine the importance of spiritual and physical discipline which leads to godly revival and awakening."

John nodded and whispered to his mother, "We were talking about this yesterday."

"God does not punish his people" Jonathan said. "Sometimes he chooses to discipline them and refine their character, but it was Jesus Christ who paid the ultimate punishment for our sins. It was Christ who stood before an angry God and took the punishment in our place. It was Christ and Christ alone who satisfied the wrath that our sins provoked. And so, when we find ourselves struggling with temptations, let us remember that either we will discipline ourselves or God will. If you truly are a Christian this morning, I encourage you to discipline yourselves before Almighty God. Pray harder, fast longer, and train your spirits to be sensitive to the voice of God."

The congregation was amazed. They had never heard a preacher so young with so deep and sincere a message. His words were powerful, yet spoken softly and with great reservation. Every once in a while, Jonathan would glance up from his manuscript to look into the eyes of the people, but for most of the sermon, he kept his face glued to his text and faithfully read what God had given him to say.

Jonathan continued. "Like the waves against a boat, Christians will rock back and forth between discipline and laziness. One day we will find ourselves right with God and seeking the way of holiness, and on another day we will be in the depths, seeking and striving after the passions of our flesh. Yet, it is comforting to realize that Christ himself is with us. Whenever we feel tempted, Christ is there, remembering his own temptation while he was on earth. Whenever we feel lonely, Christ is there, wrapping his arms around us and reminding us that heaven is on the horizon. And, of course, whenever we sin, Christ is there, watching us provoke the Lord to wrath."

Every member of the congregation was wide-eyed and thinking about the times in their lives that they had sinned. "Was Christ really there when I stole that piece of taffy?" a child asked his mother. She nodded and told him to continue listening to the sermon.

"But thanks be to God," Jonathan said. "That we are not left to ourselves. Thanks be to God that the Creator has not abandoned his creation after we sin against him." Jonathan looked up from his manuscript. His eyes were warm and serious. "Like the Old Testament Israelites who were led into the Promised Land, God has brought our ancestors to the New World. But when we stray from his covenant, when we grow lazy in our faith, judgment will come to us like it came to those Israelites who forgot that 'he who ignores discipline despises himself, but whoever heeds correction gains understanding.' So let us give ourselves completely to God, both in action and in attitude. And may we thank our Father for disciplining his children instead of punishing us."

After the service concluded, everyone in the congregation wanted to shake his hand. "Good message, young man," some said. "I pray God will make you our permanent pastor," another said. One woman approached him with tears in her eyes. "Please pray for my oldest son," she pleaded. "He does not know God and I fear that his soul is fixed on rebellion." Another said, "And also pray for my brother. He is addicted to card playing and alcohol. I fear that he will be taken from this world any moment and never see the glory and grace of God."

Jonathan continued to speak to each member of the congregation. Their needs became his needs, their prayers, his prayers. And as he talked with them he began to love them more and more. "It would be an honor to be the pastor of this church," he told John on the way home. "The members seem serious about their calling as Christians and if God leads, I would very much like to stay here in New York."

"You told me yourself," John replied, "that the wind of God guides our ships. Perhaps you should lower your sails since God has led you here."

Jonathan shook his head. "Someone once told me that God does not send us without going with us. I sense God is here with me in New York, walking with me by the docks and teaching me to discipline myself as Christians should. As much as I would like to lower my sails, I think I'll leave them up, just in case the wind picks up again."

Cured by Sickness

North Haven, Connecticut, 1725

KNOCK! KNOCK! KNOCK! Esther Edwards beat her fists against the door.

"You must be his mother," Isaac Stiles said, opening the door. "Please come in."

"I came as quickly as I could," she said. "What happened?"

Isaac led Esther to the bedroom where Jonathan was staying. "He was walking through the woods and he collapsed," he said. "A woodsman found him lying near a tree and brought him to me. Since we were childhood friends, I thought it would be okay if he stayed in my house. I think he is far too sick to be moved."

Esther placed her hand against Jonathan's head. "He's burning up," she said, placing a wet rag on his brow. "How long has he been sleeping?"

"Three days," Isaac said. "I've tried to wake him up several times because he needs to eat something, but he hasn't opened an eye since he was found. He's very ill and needs constant attention. The doctor came by yesterday and told us to watch him at all hours, especially through the night."

America's Genius

Esther hated to see her son so sick. Several years prior, she had visited him in college when he was plagued by pleurisy, but he looked even worse now. "Jonathan has moved several times this year," she said. "After he left New York, he went to Yale University to be a tutor. Then he was invited to be the pastor of a small town called Bolton. Have you heard of it?"

"Why yes," Isaac said. "That's the new town settled by the people of Windsor. Coming from New York to Bolton must have been a hard transition. Bolton is just a small country village."

"It was a hard decision to make because he really enjoyed preaching at the church by the docks, but he sensed God leading him away."

"Tell me about his responsibilities as a tutor," Isaac said. "I've heard that can be exhausting and could explain his collapse."

"You have to understand that my son is by nature a hard worker. If his day is empty, he will fill it with studying nature, sketching, or practicing spiritual disciplines. So when he agreed to take the position as tutor, I knew he would enjoy the busy schedule. But perhaps he worked too hard. I know that Yale paid him extra for organizing and cataloging their library on top of guest lecturing in classrooms and helping students understand their homework."

"What did a typical day look like for him?" Isaac asked.

"Well, it started at sunrise with a chapel service. Then Jonathan taught two or three classes during the morning. He broke for lunch at noon, attending evening prayers from 4:00 p.m. to 5:00 p.m., went to dinner after that and studied until 11:00 p.m. It is a challenging schedule for anyone his age."

While Esther was speaking, Isaac pulled a bag from under the bed and handed it to her. "This is what Jonathan was carrying when he was found. I didn't want to examine its contents before you arrived."

Esther untied the leather strings and pulled out two books and a stack of papers. "These must be what he is studying," she said. One by one she examined, *William Ames' Cases of Conscience*, John Locke's *Essay Concerning Human Understanding*, and two sermons he had written, *The Pleasantness of Religion*, and *Nothing Upon Earth Can Represent the Glories of Heaven*. Esther placed the papers and books back on the desk and turned back to speak to Isaac. "After Jonathan graduated with his Master's Degree he was invited to be the pastor at Bolton. Well his congregation was always fighting about something and were not a happy people." She continued to talk while sitting by her son's bedside. "Jonathan tried to think positively about his time there and his sermons were always good, but he once told me in a letter that the members of his church were like sheep, devouring one another. It was a blessing when Yale offered him the position of Tutor of the College."

"Could there have been anything else that might have contributed to his collapse?" Isaac asked.

Esther sighed. "He did tell me that he was struggling spiritually. He said that he felt numb on the inside and that his faith was falling apart. I never heard him talk like this before, but assumed that God would give him the grace to get over his depression."

KNOCK! KNOCK! KNOCK!

"Who could that be?" Isaac asked, walking to the door. Isaac grabbed his deer hunting rifle and slowly opened the door.

A young girl with dark hair looked up at him. She wore a plain, blue dress that was fringed at the bottom. "My name is Sarah Pierpont," she said, "and I have come to see Jonathan."

Isaac put his gun away and invited her inside. "How did you know that Jonathan was here?" he asked.

"Timothy Edwards told me," she replied. "Now, please, take me to him."

Isaac led Sarah to the room where Esther and Jonathan were. Tears welled up in her eyes when she saw Jonathan lying on the bed. His skin was pale and she had never seen him like this before. Sarah looked at Esther. "Jonathan has told me all about you. It's a pleasure to finally meet you," she said.

"How do you know my son?" Esther asked.

"When Jonathan was in college at Wethersfield he went to my father's church, New Haven's First Church. At the time I was only thirteen years old, but we became friends. My great grandfather was Thomas Hooker, the founder of Hartford."

Jonathan Edwards

"And you and Jonathan have been spending some time together lately?" Esther asked, suspiciously.

Sarah smiled. "You could say that. I brought a poem he wrote to me not long ago. Would you like to read it?"

Esther nodded and Sarah handed her a folded piece of paper.

They say there is a young lady in New Haven
Whose mind is strangely sweet.
She has an uncommon purity in her affections;
Is most just and praiseworthy in all her actions;
And you could not persuade her
To do anything wrong or sinful.
She is the calmest and kindest girl in all the world.

"This is Jonathan's handwriting," Esther said. "And if what this poem says about you is true, then I am more than happy that he is spending time with you."

Suddenly, Jonathan opened his eyes.

"Jonathan!" Isaac said, rushing over to the bed.

"Where am I?" he asked.

Sarah and Esther grabbed his hand. "You're safe," Esther said. "Your friend, Isaac Stiles, has been taking care of you in his house. You collapsed in the field. Don't you remember?"

Jonathan closed his eyes and tried to remember. "I remember leaving Yale to visit you and Father in East Windsor. I remember walking through the forest and… I think there was a spider. Yes, it was brown and red and unlike any I have ever seen. I climbed up the trunk of a tree to get a closer look. That's all I remember."

"You must have fallen," Isaac said. "It's a good thing you were found. You might not have woken up out there."

"I'm starving," Jonathan said, sitting up in the bed.

"You haven't eaten anything in three days," his mother said. "I will go make you some soup." Esther kissed his forehead and went into the kitchen.

Sarah wrapped her arms around his neck. "I'm so glad you are okay," she said.

Jonathan raised his eyebrows. "I'm sorry, have we met?"

Sarah looked confused. "Of course we've met," she said. "Jonathan, it's me, Sarah. We met while you were going to college several years ago. Remember how we walked through the woods? You told me about God and his grace and I told you about how to make apple dumplings. Don't you remember me?"

Jonathan couldn't remember, but pretended to anyway. "I must have hit my head, I don't remember much of anything."

"The doctor said that might happen," Isaac announced. "He said that if you suffered memory loss it would come back to you shortly after you awoke."

Jonathan was terrified. If there was one thing in his life he didn't want to lose, it was his memory. To forget about his friends would be terrible, but to forget about his Savior would be hell. "Sarah, if you know me like you say, ask me questions about my faith."

Sarah thought for a moment. They had only talked two or three times about serious matters. "Very well, here's one. Who was John Calvin and what did he believe?"

Jonathan scratched his head. "John Calvin was a sixteenth-century Swiss theologian who emphasized God's absolute control and taught that from before the foundations of the world God chose to save his people from eternal destruction."

Sarah, who often talked to her father about the reformation, had never heard such a brilliant summary of John Calvin's view of Scripture. "And who was Jacobus Arminius?" she asked.

"These are easy questions, Sarah, ask me something harder."

Sarah wouldn't. "Not until you answer my question," she said with a smirk.

"Fine," Jonathan replied. "Jacobus Arminius was a sixteenth-century Dutch Protestant theologian who believed that people retain a natural ability to choose God's grace or to resist it."

"Very good!" Sarah said. "Now which one do you believe?"

Jonathan paused. "Well, I don't remember," he said. "I suppose it would make me feel happy to believe that humans were good enough to choose God, but the Bible says the opposite. The Bible says that we love God because he first loved us. It says that no one has the natural ability to choose God without God first choosing us. Besides, God told Jeremiah, 'Before I formed you in the womb I knew you, before you were born I set you apart; I appointed you as a prophet to the nations. Jeremiah 1:5.' Now I might have lost some memory, Sarah, but it sounds like God not only chose him, but also formed him and sustained him to be his messenger. Well! I do believe I'm getting my memory back!"

"Do you remember me, yet?" Sarah asked.

Jonathan thought hard. He remembered going to college and studying nature and science. "Perhaps if we took a walk together I'd remember," he said. "After all, I need to get some fresh air."

It was agreed by Isaac and Esther that a short walk close to the house would not cause any harm so Jonathan was helped out of bed and they went outside. Soon the two young people found themselves in a quiet part of the garden as Esther and Isaac chatted out of sight, but not far away.

Jonathan had not walked in three days and as she supported his weight with her arm, Sarah exclaimed at the beautiful sunset.

"It's like God has dipped the clouds in paint," Jonathan agreed. Just then he looked at Sarah. "You are strangely familiar. How much time have we been spending together?"

"You asked my father if we could court about two years ago," she said.

"And what did he say?"

Sarah smiled. "You tell me."

Jonathan struggled to remember. Then his struggling stopped. "He told me that I was the only man in the whole world he would say yes to. Sarah, I remember everything! I remember you and our walks and the poems I wrote. And... before I fell I remember being terribly depressed. I hit a spiritual doldrum and no longer wanted to pray or read my Bible. Yes, I remember now. I did not want to even think about God, much less serve him."

"How do you feel now?" Sarah asked.

"I feel like a new man. The fear of dying has awakened heavenly appetites within me and I am once again seeking to serve God with all my heart. I believe God has just cured me with sickness."

Jonathan took Sarah by the hand and led her to a nearby tree. He often sat beneath trees like these and sketched bugs and stones. They intrigued him because he saw God's beauty displayed through them. But today, beauty took a different form and Jonathan sat Sarah down at the base of the trunk. "There was one more thing I just remembered," he said.

Sarah leaned against the bark. "Is it another spiritual insight about nature?" she asked.

Jonathan shook his head.

"Perhaps the secret to holiness?" she asked.

"No, that's not it either," he said. Jonathan slid his hand in hers. This was the first time he had ever done this. "Sarah Pierpont, will you marry me?"

Sarah was speechless. Even though they had courted for two years with her father's permission, she didn't expect a proposal so soon. She was only fifteen years old and none of her friends were married. She looked into Jonathan's eyes. They were determined eyes, old eyes, much older than the twenty-one year old body that held them. "Of course I'll marry you," Sarah replied.

For the first time since he could remember, Jonathan leapt in the air. His wild emotions finally overtook his calm intellect and he escorted Sarah back to Isaac's cabin. "The wedding will be in two years," he said.

"Of course," Sarah replied. "Most girls marry at twenty-three years old, but since you and my father have talked this through, I trust that God will bless our early marriage."

As they walked through the woods, Jonathan called to mind a Bible verse he had not thought about in years. "1 Timothy 1:17 says, 'Now unto the King eternal, invisible, the only wise God, be honor and glory forever and ever, Amen.' Sarah, do you believe that the all-wise, eternal God chose us to be together before the world began?"

"I've never thought about that before," she said. "But if God really is in control, then it would make sense that he created us and ordained us for each other. That makes our relationship more special than I thought. Jonathan, I'm glad you don't believe in accidents."

Jonathan watched as the sun dipped below the tree line. "Everything has a purpose," he said. "And if the earth obeys God by spinning around the sun, as Copernicus discovered, how much more should we, who live on the earth, obey him? Sarah, God put you in my life for a reason and I know that we are going to serve him better together than we ever could have by ourselves."

Judgment Day

Northampton, Connecticut, October 29, 1727

"When the people of Nineveh heard of God's wrath against them," Jonathan preached, "they tore their clothes and repented. They fell before Almighty God in prayer and fasting."

Several teenagers snickered in the back of the sanctuary. It was dark outside, being a Sunday evening, but Jonathan could see their expressions. They were mocking his words and worse, the Bible. He ignored them and continued his sermon. "Like the people of Nineveh, we also need true reformation. I have heard that many who gather here this evening have loose morals and are leading drunken lives. Judgment is coming to us if we do not get on our knees and ask God to show us his mercy."

One teenager scribbled a picture onto a piece of paper and passed it down the pew. One by one, the boys laughed as they saw it. Though his new church had over one thousand members in attendance on Sunday, Jonathan knew that a handful of mischievous boys could threaten the whole service. He once was one of them.

"There are some of us," he continued, "who care little for our souls." Jonathan's dark, penetrating eyes stared at the group of boys in the back. "We come to church every week, but curse Christ to his face by showing no respect for God by participating in idle chatter and foolish talk during the sermon."

The teenagers grew hysterical. They drew more pictures and passed them around.

"Do not be fooled, dear congregation. Were it not for the beautiful grace of God, we would all pursue the passions that lead us straight to hell. I implore you this evening to take seriously your faith and humble yourselves before the One who keeps you from falling into the lake of fire."

Suddenly, the boys grew silent. Their eyes were fixed on Pastor Edwards as he continued to preach. The pew beneath them began to vibrate. "What's going on?" they whispered.

"I burned my hand on a stove, once," Jonathan preached. "Never have I felt more pain and agony than that. Immediately, I retracted my hand as my skin began to melt on the hot iron." Jonathan closed his Bible and held out his hand to show the church his scar. "Hell will be hotter than that! And once you are there, you cannot ever leave. It is hotter than the surface of the sun, a volcanic place where lava flows, a fire so hot that it is beyond what we can ever imagine."

The teenagers dropped the pieces of paper on the ground and grew afraid. The vibration beneath their pews increased. "God's wrath is upon us," one of them yelled. Others shouted and stood to their feet.

"Guard well your souls this day," Edwards continued. "For we are not promised another. Trust in Jesus and depend on his grace and God will save you from an eternity without him."

The floor began to shake. "It's an earthquake!" someone screamed. Suddenly, the walls began to rock back and forth and the dust fell from the ceiling.

"Help!" a woman yelled as windows shattered and crashed near her head. Jonathan rushed down and helped the woman, along with some of the men from the congregation. Jonathan knew that his church could withstand the tremor. He had never felt an earthquake before, but he had studied them. As a child he read many books about the phenomenon and he knew about the pressures that fight beneath the ground. He knew that there were certain places in the world that were more likely to experience earthquakes, but never had he known about one striking New England. "What is the state of your souls this night?" Jonathan exclaimed.

"God forgive me!" some confessed. "Forgive me for lying to Ezekiel about the price of the land."

Some ran out of the church, but most stumbled down the aisle of the church, repenting of their sins and asking God to save them. At the front were the boys from the back who had misbehaved. "Forgive me, too, God for hitting Michael in the face last week."

"And me," another said, "for stealing the apples."

The boy who had drawn the picture fell on his knees before Jonathan and began to cry. "God, forgive my soul, too, for cursing you in this church tonight. Don't send me to hell in this earthquake."

The church slowly stopped shaking and Jonathan returned to the pulpit. "There are no accidents in life," he resumed. "Everything happens for a reason. And God has sent us a sign from heaven tonight to show us that we must trust in him or perish forever.

After the service was over, Jonathan and Sarah walked to their house. Sarah took her daughter's hand and led her down King Street where their house was located. "Jonathan, do you really think it was a good idea to come to Northampton?" Sarah asked.

"I do not know if it was a good idea," Jonathan replied. "But I do know that God has led us here. As you know, my grandfather needed an assistant to help him with his pastoral duties. Since he is in his eighties and very ill, he recommended me to fill the position."

The moonlight illuminated the entrance of their farm as Jonathan led his family through the main gate. "The church bought us ten acres of land," he said, "not to mention the forty acres across town to use as farmland. They are paying me well so I can provide for you and little Sarah."

"I know that God has brought us here," Sarah said, "but I've never felt an earthquake before. Do you think it is a bad sign?"

Jonathan took Sarah's hand and led her to the barn behind their house. Several families in the area recognized that Jonathan's family needed a barn, so they had pitched in and begun building it for them. Its roof was not yet constructed and the barn door lay on the ground, but it was a blessing from heaven for the Edwards family.

"Great movement always generates great friction," he said. "We should not run away from difficult situations, even earthquakes, because whenever God is at work in this world building his kingdom and saving his people, Satan is there too, trying to tear down our faith."

"There are several people in the congregation who do not believe you should speak about hell the way you do. They told me that you should also stop speaking about Satan because it scares them and their children."

Jonathan turned to his wife. "Jesus spoke more about hell than heaven," he said. "I love my congregation too much to avoid talking about it. And when my people understand the seriousness of their sin and the dangers of dying without knowing God, only then will they be ready to appreciate the depth of grace that God has lavished on his people."

Sarah nodded. She loved to hear Jonathan talk about God and faith, but she also had her doubts. She often struggled to understand the Bible, particularly the Old Testament. She couldn't understand how Jesus walked on water or fed five thousand people with one lunch, or any of the miracles in the gospels. She did a lot of doubting, but every time she talked to Jonathan, her faith was fueled to know God more deeply. She could always depend on Jonathan's relationship with God to encourage her own.

But she also worried that the church at Northampton was far too big for her husband to pastor. It was larger than anything Jonathan had preached in and she also knew how ambitious her husband was with his writing projects. He had often disclosed to her the next book he would write and she never understood how he had time to write them. "But I know that God is in control, Jonathan" she said to him at last. "And I believe that God will accomplish his will through you in this town."

Suddenly, the ground began to shake.

"Another earthquake!" Sarah shrieked. Some of the wooden planks of the barn squeaked and fell to the ground. Jonathan grabbed his wife and daughter and ran to a nearby patch of grass where there were no trees or buildings. "Lie down here," he instructed. "They call these 'aftershocks' and there will probably be many more in the next few days." Sarah obeyed and fell face first into the tall grass. Jonathan could feel the ground quake and rumble beneath them, almost as if the stomach of the earth was upset. "Preserve our lives, oh God," he prayed, "according to your good and pleasing will." In the distance he saw oak trees fall and crash against the ground. The whole forest quivered violently as birds flew over them, looking for a safe place to land.

"Is God's wrath worse than this?" Sarah asked, thinking about her husband's sermon.

Jonathan buried his face in the grass. "Much worse," he said. "We need a revival."

Jonathan woke up at 4:00 a.m. the next morning. He usually awoke at this hour to start off his day with prayer and Bible study. Every morning he woke up this early and spent approximately thirteen hours in his study writing, reading, and praying. Sarah usually brought him breakfast at around 9:30 a.m. and prayed with her husband for several hours.

"God," Jonathan prayed. "I pray that these earthquakes do not harm anyone in our congregation. Wrap these people with your arms of love and peace during this time of tribulation."

Sarah, who was experiencing sickness and headaches during her pregnancy, woke up earlier than normal and walked into Jonathan's office. His office was small, but orderly. Shelves of books surrounded a sturdy, wooden desk and the chair where he spent most of his time thinking and meditating. "Jonathan," she whispered. "What are you reading?"

Jonathan put the book aside and turned to speak to his wife. "It's called *The Day of Doom*," he told her. "It was written in 1662 by a man named Michael Wigglesworth and it speaks about the end of times."

Sarah picked it up. "It looks dreadful," she said.

"That it is," Jonathan replied, "but many people are reading it and it has become a best seller on both sides of the Atlantic."

"Tell me how your writing projects are coming on."

Jonathan had bitten off more than he could chew with his pastoral duties, but he knew that God was calling him to write several major books. "Even at this hour," he said, "I have been planning on writing a book about God for those who do not know him."

Sarah loved hearing about her husband's projects. She loved the way he gave God the glory for his work and would not consider doing anything without fervent and faithful prayer. She also enjoyed watching Jonathan read. His brain was like a sponge and he remembered everything he soaked up. When they first married, they often stayed up late at night and talked about what they had read.

"Several mothers in our congregation approached me last week. They were deeply concerned about their teenagers."

Jonathan was curious. "What have they been doing?" he asked.

"It's called 'bundling' and it's a new practice sweeping through New England," she said.

"Bundling?" Jonathan asked. "I've not heard of it."

Sarah sighed and sat down beside her husband. "It's scandalous, Jonathan, and most of the parents permit it to happen. Bundling is when several teenagers, both male and female, get into bed together with all their clothes on and fall asleep."

Jonathan could not believe his ears. "What is the purpose of this practice?" he asked.

"That was my question to their parents," Sarah replied. "The parents these days believe that it is best to be less strict with their children and are allowing them to do many ungodly things. But some of the parents raised serious questions as to the morality of their decisions and wanted to bring it to my attention."

"I will have a word with the congregation about it," he said, shaking his head. "I believe there is not a country in this world where parents indulge their children in such wicked ways than in our own land. I'm sure the parents in our church believe that their teenagers will have the power to resist sexual temptation, but this practice must stop. We who profess to be Christian must act like Christians, for our own sake, and for the sake of the world."

Sarah nodded. "I was reading the book of Psalms just yesterday," she said. Sarah reached out for Jonathan's leather Bible and turned to Psalm 101:4. "I will have nothing to do with evil," she read. "When teenagers get into bed together, even if they do not intend to give themselves to sexual pleasure, it gives the appearance of evil."

Jonathan agreed. "And Ephesians 5 3 says, 'But among you there must not be even a hint of sexual immorality.' I have noticed lately how unmarried pregnancies have increased throughout New England. In fact, I was just talking with a pastor in Boston about the subject. He told me that, in his area, many young people were having sex before marriage and that he was trying to abolish it in his church."

Sarah stood up to leave. "I fear for the destiny of the younger generation," she said.

Jonathan did too. He remembered his school days and how even his own generation developed a strong taste for immorality. "God," he prayed, "preserve our young people and teach them your ways. Invigorate them to know you and love you because you know and love them. They are like sheep and you are their shepherd. Protect them from the wolves that seek their lives. And give me the wisdom to lead your people, especially during this difficult season."

Several hours later, Jonathan heard a knock at the door. Sarah opened it.

"Well, hello," Solomon Stoddard said.

"Please come in," Sarah said, leading him to Jonathan's study.

"Grandfather!" Jonathan said, standing to his feet. Since Jonathan and his grandfather were both fulfilling their duties as pastor of the church in Northampton, they often spent time together.

"Young man," Solomon said, "I have lived a long life. I have seen many things and known many people." Solomon coughed several times.

"Are you well?" Jonathan asked.

"No, my time on this earth is almost through, but I wanted to share something with you." Jonathan listened intently. His grandfather was one of a very few people who had a great influence over Jonathan's life.

"As you know," Solomon said, "the spiritual climate of our community is falling."

"Yes", Jonathan replied, "just this morning, my wife was telling me about that."

Solomon leaned back in his chair. "It is worse than you think," he said. "Several of our members have tried to kill themselves. One of them succeeded. His name is Joseph Hawley and he slit his throat with a knife."

Jonathan's jaw dropped. "Why did he do this?"

"He was suffering from depression," Solomon replied. "His family said that he had fallen into a terrible state. He could not think clearly, he could not talk clearly, and the doctor said that he was delirious. He was only forty-two years old."

Jonathan's heart sank. "Satan seems to be in a great rage at this extraordinary breaking out of God's truth," he said. "I hope it is because he knows that his time is short."

"Oh, he knows," Solomon said. "The ancient dragon remembers when he was thrown out of heaven. He knows that in the end, God will punish him forever for his rebellion. But in the meantime I want you to remember something. Christians must go back to the past in order to go forward into the future. We must go back to the Bible, to its history, to our own history. We must know where we came from and how we suffered.

America's Genius

We must understand the great heroes of the faith who have risked everything for the sake of the gospel. Only then can we be prepared to fight the world, the flesh, and the devil."

Jonathan had never heard anyone say that before. He was a great student of history, particularly Christian history. He loved to study how the Protestant Reformers discovered that the grace of God was a free gift and how they carefully translated the Bible so everyone could read it for themselves. After listening to his grandfather, it all made sense to him. Everything he learned about the past prepared him for the future."

"Say," Solomon said, "I was reading the other day about a fellow named Benjamin Franklin. He's a scientist who claims that he is on the verge of understanding the power of lightning. And he believes that it can be harnessed and controlled."

Jonathan laughed. "Lightning? Controlled? That's impossible!" After several seconds of thought, Jonathan corrected himself. "No, it might actually be possible. God gave us permission to govern the world, so perhaps we can govern lightning too."

Solomon knew that God had equipped Jonathan with brilliancy and faithfulness. That's the reason he decided to call him to the church to be his pastoral assistant. "Now, Jonathan," he said. "We must pray that God sends a lightning of revival to our church. We cannot harness or control the movement of God's presence, but we can certainly pray for it. I am going to preach this Sunday and I would like you to spend the week in prayer and fasting. Pray about how best to handle the immorality of the youth. Pray about how to comfort the family of Joseph Hawley. And I will be praying that your prayers will be heard."

Jonathan helped Solomon to his feet. "I will do as you ask," he said, handing him his cane.

Solomon laid his hands on Jonathan's shoulder. "Son," he said, "listen to me carefully. There are times when God raises up servants to proclaim his truth. These people preach God's Word even when it is not the popular message. They resist the temptation to keep God's Word to themselves and bravely announce the light of Christ to a dark and dying society. You, Jonathan, are one of these people. God has raised you up as a lighthouse in this land. Keep studying, keep praying, and most of all, never forget my words—greater is he who is in you than he who is in the world."

After a brief prayer, Solomon left and Jonathan returned to his study. The pages of his Bible were yellow and starting to wear out, but he opened it anyway. He opened it to Acts 1:8 and read the words of Jesus out loud. "But you will receive power when the Holy Spirit comes on you; and you will be my witnesses in Jerusalem, and in all Judea and Samaria, and to the ends of the earth." Jonathan had read that verse hundreds of times, but this time felt different. It felt fresh and new. "God, help me as I continue to be your witness, even here in Connecticut, at the very ends of the earth."

Awakening

Enfield, Massachusetts-Connecticut border, July 8, 1741

"The revivals have been flowing rapidly," Joseph Meacham said.

"And perhaps God will use my sermon today to continue them," Jonathan said. Joseph was the pastor at Coventry, a town not far from Northampton. Joseph, along with Stephen William and several other clergymen from Connecticut, had been traveling with Edwards around the province to fuel the awakenings that were occurring throughout New England.

"Tell us, Mr. Edwards," Stephen said, "about your time with George Whitefield."

Jonathan thought about the previous year when Whitefield came to New England on a preaching tour. "He is a young man," Jonathan said. "Only twenty-five years old. But his voice can be heard from over a mile away."

"Is it true what they said about Benjamin Franklin's experiments on him?" Joseph asked.

Jonathan nodded. "Not only is it true, it is downright miraculous. Franklin tested Whitefield's voice to see how many people could hear it outdoors and he discovered that twenty-five thousand people could hear his voice at a single time. God has truly blessed young Whitefield and equipped him to be a revolutionary preacher."

"How long did he stay in your home?" Stephen asked.

"When Whitefield came to our church in Northampton we were privileged to host him for several days. He spoke to my children about the things of God and my daughter, Jerusha, even received the Lord into her life."

"And tell us more about his preaching style," Stephen insisted.

Jonathan paused. "He and I are very different," he eventually said. "You see, Whitefield is a very emotional preacher, often swinging his hands in the air, preaching without notes, and weeping during every sermon. He is far more energetic than I am, but I sensed a common passion for Christ and an undying ambition to serve the Lord. I do confess, that when he began to preach in my church about revival, I too wept along with the entirety of my congregation."

Stephen wanted to know more. "I heard that when he preached in Boston, he gathered twenty-thousand people together to hear his sermon. Never has a crowd that large gathered anywhere in the colonies before."

"Not long ago," Jonathan said, "Whitefield wrote me a letter in which he told me that Benjamin Franklin had asked him if they wanted to go to Ohio and start a colony that would be a better example of Christianity to the Indians than what we have here in Connecticut."

The clergymen looked astonished. "But Franklin and Whitefield do not see eye-to-eye on God."

"That is true," Jonathan continued. "But even despite their differences, it is amazing how Whitefield impressed even the talented and famous Benjamin Franklin. You know, before he left for England, I took a walk with Whitefield and told him about my reluctance to preach as he does, with such emotion. I do not think he appreciated me saying that, even though he responded with great kindness."

"Yes," Stephen said. "That's what I like about you, Jonathan. You never put politeness over principles. And now, let us pray for you as you prepare to preach the gospel here in Enfield." Several clergymen gathered around him as Stephen led the prayer. "God, we ask that you uplift your servant, Jonathan, this day. You have given him a word from your lips to be delivered to your people and we ask that they might receive it with open ears and hearts. We pray, particularly for the topic of the sermon that it might convey your truth to those who know only lies. Amen." Stephen stopped praying and whispered to Jonathan, "What is the topic?"

Jonathan answered, "Sinners in the Hands of an Angry God." Joseph looked surprised. He had never heard a title like that before, but then again, he had never heard Jonathan preach before either.

After the prayer, Jonathan and the clergymen walked onto the platform of the meetinghouse and took their seats. The entire assembly was talking vainly and thoughtlessly, even through the singing of the hymns.

"And now let us stand and sing to the Lord," Joseph said, opening Isaac Watt's *Hymns and Spiritual Songs*. Singing had been a source of controversy for many years in New England. Some said that the Puritans only needed to sing Biblical words like the Psalms set to music. Others, like Isaac Watts, believed that it was appropriate to sing sacred songs that reflect biblical themes without necessarily using the exact words of biblical passages. Jonathan, who had studied music and wrote poetry, enjoyed these new songs and their creative handling of God's eternal truths.

"Let us turn to page forty-six and sing all the stanzas of 'Jesus Shall Reign.'" Jonathan loved this song. He loved it because it portrayed the absolute sovereignty and dominion that Christ has in the world. The melody was attractive so he often sang this song in the cold winter while chopping wood in the forest behind his house.

Jesus shall reign where'er the sun,
Does his successive journeys run.
His kingdom stretch from shore to shore,
Till moons shall wax and wane no more.

After Jonathan sang the last verse, he stepped up to the pulpit. He had preached this sermon several times, beginning with his home church. This was one of his favorite sermons because it describes God's infinite love and mercy to sinners who want to rebel against him. "My text this morning is Deuteronomy 32: 5," he said, "'Their foot shall slip in due time.'"

As he began to preach, the chattering congregation grew silent. Joseph, who had led the music despite the noise of their talking, was in shock as Jonathan captivated their attention with his calm, soft voice. "Indeed, the spirit has fallen on these people," he whispered.

"Your wickedness makes you heavier than lead," Jonathan said with a soft voice. The people strained their ears to hear him. "And your weight bears down upon you, pulling you into the very bowels of hell."

The assembly had never heard a sermon like this before. The squeaking of a mouse could have been heard as Jonathan continued to speak.

"All your righteousness cannot save you any more than a spider's web can stop a rock passing though its spindle." Jonathan remembered his childhood days and how easily rocks passed through webs. "The wrath of God is like a rising water, swirling and increasing in intensity. The bow of God's anger is bent against you because of your sin and the arrow is ready on the string and nothing but the mere pleasure of God keeps the blade from being drunk with your blood."

As Jonathan's sermon gained momentum, the assembly began making noises. Strange noises. Deep noises. They had never thought that sin made God so angry before. They had never considered that their unconverted souls were in such a dangerous place as this, and they listened intently to Jonathan's words.

"The God who holds you over the pit of hell, much as one holds a spider over the fire, is dreadfully provoked by you. He is so pure and holy and you are so vile and loathsome, yet his strong and unwavering hand does not let you go. He is angry with you, and there is no reason to keep you safe, but he wraps you in his fingers so that you will not fall away. Oh sinner! Consider the fearful danger you are in."

The noises began to grow. People were coming to understand that God was not pleased with their lives and they needed to repent. Some were shrieking. Others moaned. "I've never heard such a noise," Joseph said. "They are all crying out to Jesus to save them from the wrath to come."

"God can save each and every one of you today," Jonathan concluded. "But never forget that he will give you his mercy, not because you deserve it, but because you need it." At this point, the crowd had become so hysterical that Jonathan's voice was drowned out and not even Joseph could regain control over them. Since Jonathan knew he could not be heard, they ended the service with a prayer and then the clergymen shared the gospel one-on-one with everyone who requested it.

A woman approached Jonathan. Her eyes were wet and her face was red. "My daughter asked me to give this to you." She handed him an envelope. "She insisted that I speak with you. If you have the time, Mr. Edwards, please consider writing her back."

As Jonathan spoke with each person, his head began to swirl. He had preached for thirty minutes and was exhausted. "If you will excuse me," he told the gentleman he was speaking with, "I feel as though I am going to faint." Joseph and Stephen, who had been watching Jonathan ever since he stepped down from the pulpit, escorted him out of the noisy crowd.

As the horse brought the buggy to the back entrance of the meetinghouse, Jonathan collapsed on the ground. "Hurry, open the door!" Stephen said. Joseph, who was the bigger of the men, laid Jonathan in the coach and climbed into the car with him. Stephen beat against the side of the carriage. "Make it fast, driver," he yelled. "We have a long journey ahead of us and our friend is ill."

The carriage sped away with the three men inside. "Do you think he will be alright?" Joseph asked.

Stephen tore his shirt to make a rag, dipped it into the canteen of water he had brought and laid it on Jonathan's forehead. "Jonathan once told me that he frequently lost consciousness when he over exerted himself. That sermon was unlike anything I've ever heard. I hope it is nothing more serious."

The carriage scraped against branches as it raced through the woods. The two white horses raced through the darkness, floating like mist through the trees. It was a bumpy ride, and every once in a while a back wheel would hit a rock or stump, nearly knocking the driver from his seat. But at least they were covering ground.

Jonathan awoke with a terrible headache.

"Mr. Edwards!" Stephen exclaimed. "Are you well?"

Jonathan looked out the carriage window. He could see a tree line slowly disappear into the distance. "Where am I?" he said.

"We are taking you back to Northampton," Joseph said. "You passed out after your sermon in Enfield."

"How did the congregation respond to the sermon?" Jonathan asked.

"Oh very well," Stephen replied. "There is an awakening brewing in our land and never have I seen God use a sermon to convict and convert so many souls. There were dozens of teenagers who gave their lives to God, not to mention the scores of adults who rededicated their lives. It was indeed a miracle from God and I know he used your words to increase his kingdom."

Jonathan saw an envelope lying next to him. "What's this?" he asked, picking it up. Joseph had lit an oil-burning lamp and handed it to Jonathan. As he slit the top of the envelope, he remembered the woman who handed it to him.

Dear Mr. Edwards,

We have never met, but I heard you preach at my church in Suffield not long ago after our pastor died. My name is Deborah Hatheway and God used you to convict me of my sin and persuade me to give my life to the service of Christ. When I heard that you would be preaching in Enfield I longed to attend. Unfortunately, I could not be there, but I pray my letter reaches you well.

My chief concern is that I keep going back to the sins I hate. I cannot seem to break free of them, though I want to very much. There are even times when I have fasted and prayed all night for God to take these evils from me, but I still find wicked desires and temptations too much to bear. Do you have any advice for me concerning these matters?

Most sincerely,
Deborah Hatheway

Jonathan understood her struggle with sin, for he, too, continued to battle against his flesh. Before sticking the letter back into his pocket, he tore a piece of paper from the envelope and fastened it onto his shirt button.

Stephen looked at Joseph, worried that Jonathan had lost his mind. "Mr. Edwards," he said, "May I ask why you did that?"

Jonathan smiled at his friends. "I have not plummeted into insanity," he promised. "At least, not very deeply. But I have always found it extremely beneficial to make notes upon my body to help me remember things to do or insights that cross my mind during the course of a day. For example, when I am walking along a mountain trail in the Spring and do not have time to write every thought that comes to mind, I tear a piece of paper from my pocket and stick it to my shirt."

"And what kind of things come to your mind?" Joseph asked.

"Just two days ago I was thinking about Simon Peter," Jonathan said. "I remembered how terrifying it must have been when Jesus called him to step out of his boat and walk on the water. And then a Scripture passage came to mind." Jonathan looked up into the air, almost as if reaching for the text with his mind. "Ah, yes, he remembered. Matthew 14: 30–31 reads, 'But when [Peter] saw the wind, he was afraid and, beginning to sink, cried out, "Lord, save me!" Immediately Jesus reached out his hand and caught him. "You of little faith," he said, "why did you doubt?" I wanted to remember how the strong arms of Christ reached down to save Peter when he could not save himself, so I stuck a note on my right arm so I could recollect that story and write it down when I got home."

Stephen grinned. "And why did you stick that note on your chest?" he asked.

"Because a woman has asked me how she can be a better Christian," Jonathan replied. "It is a matter of the heart and soul. I think I will write her a letter about Peter and how Christ's hand held him from falling into the depths like one would hold a spider above a puddle of water."

Joseph, who had recently preached on that text remarked, "I've never thought about it like that before, Jonathan, but I suppose that is a perfect picture of how Jesus saved his people. He shows us a restraining grace, a grace that does not let us fall when all our sin would sink us quickly. And before we have a chance to grab anything, God grabs us and pulls us to himself."

Before too long the carriage had arrived at Jonathan's home. Fond farewells were said as Jonathan waved his friends on their way to their own homes. Walking through the door of his own house, he was greeted by Sarah with a huge hug. She had stayed up late waiting for him while the children were sleeping. "How was your sermon?" she asked.

Jonathan put his bag against the wall. "The Lord was honored through it," he said. "And many surrendered their souls to God. One lady even wrote to me and asked me to give her advice concerning the edification of her faith. A great awakening is bursting forth throughout New England. People are recognizing their own helplessness and are trusting in Christ for their salvation. As you know, for years I have prayed that God would accomplish an outpouring of his spirit upon our land, and I believe he is answering those prayers in ways I could not even have imagined."

"Revival has been breaking out in our town, too," Sarah said, excitedly. "The teenagers in our church have all professed their faith in Christ and have vowed to live in a way that pleases God. Since you left on your preaching tour, we have had ten more people join our church. God is doing great and mighty things in this town and he is using you as his instrument. Now get some sleep and I will bring you breakfast in the morning."

Jonathan kissed Sarah goodnight and walked into his study. By the flickering of a candle, he took a piece of paper and a cup of ink and placed them on his desk. His feather pen was light in his hand, but it would soon feel much heavier. He had weighty things to write about.

Dear Miss Hatheway,

I thank you very much for your kind words, Deborah, and am grateful to God that he has worked wonders in your life by drawing you to his side. Concerning your letter, I would like to give you several pieces of advice. First of all, the Christian life is not smooth. To be a believer in Jesus Christ is a call to die. We must die to our sinful pleasures and wicked appetites. We must die to our pride, which is the worst viper of the heart. It strikes at every moment and must be destroyed daily. Pride was the first sin that ever was and is most difficult to root out of us. You expressed that you are having trouble ridding yourself of sin. Continue to press on towards Christ, never give up. Fight your temptation for sinfulness with a temptation for holiness. Wake up every morning and feel your great unworthiness before God. Only then will you be able to seek first God's kingdom and progress as a pilgrim in this land.

Sincerely,
Jonathan Edwards

Last of the Mohicans

Stockbridge, Massachusetts, August 16, 1751

A violent storm swirled over Jonathan's head as he walked beside Chief Hendrick through the mountains near Stockbridge village. Chief Hendrick was a well-known Mohawk leader who had become a Christian, traveled widely, and held a great respect for the English colonists. He had dark brown eyes and black hair. He often wore a headdress of feathers and bones, and unlike Jonathan's pale complexion, Chief Hendrick had tan skin.

"Tell me," Hendrick said, "Why did you leave your church in Northampton to come and preach to the Mohawks and Mohicans here in Stockbridge?"

"My family and I were forced out of the church," Jonathan said.

Chief Hendrick could see that the wounds were still fresh on Jonathan's mind. "Why would any congregation want you to leave? You are an international preacher and writer. Even we Mohawks have heard of you through our friend David Brainerd."

"There was a scandal in my community," Jonathan said. "Several boys conducted themselves inappropriately towards some of the girls in our church and many people thought I over-reacted by disciplining them too severely. The church also felt that Sarah and I were being paid too much every year. Our house is more of a hotel than a home because we have so many visitors and we always cover the expenses of our guests. Northampton has become a very secular town, and after twenty-three years of ministry, my church found enough excuses to remove me for preaching the gospel."

"That must have been difficult," Hendrick said. "But I am glad the Lord was pleased to send you our way."

"As am I," Jonathan replied. "The Lord moves in mysterious ways. He often closes doors so we will walk through the open ones. Since Sarah and I no longer have as large an income as we did at Northampton, our girls have become creative. They are making fans and other useful crafts that can be sold. Your tribe has taught them much about how to be resourceful with the land and I know they are grateful."

"My people have always respected the land," Chief said. "Perhaps we have respected it too much—even to the point of worshipping it."

"I've read much about the Mohican and Mohawk tribes and how they have a great respect for animals and nature. As you say, they respect and worship the land, but such adoration can also be a bridge that links the gospel to their lives. Ever since my childhood I've been interested in evangelizing the Indian tribes in New England. As a boy, I drew insects and animals, trying to learn all I could about how they worked. Even to this day I see God's hand at work in creation. Even the smallest leaf testifies to God's creativity in shaping it. Perhaps God put those desires in me for a reason. Perhaps they will equip me to minister to the residents of Stockbridge."

"We have a very new community," Hendrick said. "Stockbridge was founded in 1730 by English colonists who wanted to evangelize Mohicans. Mohicans were once a very powerful and dominating presence in this land, but since the Mohican confederacy dissolved, only a remnant remains."

Jonathan shook his head. "I've heard stories about how the Mohicans were not treated very well."

The chief nodded. "But ever since the Europeans conquered this territory, the Mohicans sensed that times were changing and some of the leaders sent their children to be educated by the English colonists here at Stockbridge. They decided that education is the only way to survive in this changing world and it has been a blessing being able to watch Mohicans, Mohawks, and English puritans live here in peace."

Stockbridge had impressed Jonathan for many reasons, even when he was serving as the pastor at Northampton. He knew that the leaders of the city cared deeply for the souls of the Mohicans and were teaching them English. He loved that Mohican children were coming to know the Lord and reading the Bible for themselves.

"I believe God will save many souls in this town," Jonathan said, looking at it over the Housatonic River. "It is a prototype for future missions where people of different backgrounds and traditions live in harmony. In fact, it is the very picture of heaven." Jonathan remembered what John saw on the island of Patmos in Revelation 7: 9. He recited the verse aloud to Chief Hendrick: "After this I looked and there before me was a great multitude that no one could count, from every nation, tribe, people and language, standing before the throne and in front of the Lamb."

"It is strange for a Mohawk to accept the idea of heaven," Chief Hendrick said. "For me, that was one of the hardest concepts to understand because in our tribe we believe that our souls become one with animals and nature. Yet, I must confess, when God came into my heart and life, I have many times thought of heaven as being a place of eternal rest and happiness."

Jonathan looked at the dark clouds above the mountains. "Yes, it will be that, but it will be more than that," he said. "It will be a place of worship, where we forever glorify the God who came down to us and purchased us with his blood. It is hard, I suppose, to even wrap our minds around the concept of worshipping God forever because we are viewing it through selfish eyes. But in heaven, we will not be tempted to sin. There will be no sin at all and we will be the happiest because God is before our eyes."

As Jonathan and Chief Hendrick walked through the town gate, Timothy, one of Jonathan's sons, ran by. "I see your children have already become friends with our children," the Chief said, watching his son run beside Timothy.

Jonathan smiled. "Timothy rarely speaks English any more," he said. "He even told me that he thinks in your original language. Perhaps God will use him one day to advance his kingdom and bring many people to know and love Jesus."

"I had a conversation with David Brainerd about you once," Hendrick said. "It was Brainerd who led me to the Lord and he had many nice things to say about you. How long did you know him?"

"David and I were great friends," Jonathan said. "He was so young and full of zeal when I met him. In 1747, he came to stay with us in Northampton. Soldiers who had been fighting the Indians occupied our house and when he arrived, our house was still blockaded. Every day was a blessing to be alive. David had already established himself as a great missionary to the Indians and it broke his heart to witness the war against them."

"How did David meet the Lord?" Chief asked.

"When he was twenty-one years old," Jonathan said, "David felt God tugging on his soul when he attended Yale College. He gave his life to Christian missionary work. Though he did not have a license to preach here in Connecticut, a society in Scotland for Propagating Christian Knowledge supported him as he worked in the Mohican village of Kaunemeek, which is twenty miles from Stockbridge. He then traveled to Delaware to minister to the tribes there, but while he was preaching at Crossweeksung, he collapsed, too sick to continue. Not long after that, he came to our house where he eventually died. One of our daughters, Jerusha, loved him very much and four months later, she died too. I buried them next to each other, as Jerusha wanted."

"I have heard that you wrote a biography of David Brainerd after he died," Chief said. "I have not yet read it, but I know that it has helped our people come to understand the gospel of Christ."

As they were talking, rain began to fall upon Stockbridge. Both Puritans and Indians fled for shelter as lightning streaked through the sky. The children who had been playing leapfrog in the cornfields retraced their steps through the tall crops as the water stung against their faces. It was a good day to be inside.

"Repeat after me," Sarah Edwards said. "Water."

The four and five-year-old Mohawks repeated the word.

"House," Sarah said next, watching them open their mouths wide to let the word come out. The Mohican and Mohawk children spoke English well, but Sarah

Jonathan Edwards

wanted to make sure they sounded out each and every syllable. Words were important things and to be able to communicate was the best skill anyone could have.

Like her husband, Sarah demanded perfection. Ever since Jonathan brought his family to Stockbridge, Sarah ministered to the wives and children of the Indians. She wanted them to be as prepared as possible to face the dangerous future and that meant mastering the English language. Every day she labored with them, teaching them mathematics and science, not to mention Bible stories and parables. Before they arrived, only boys were being taught to read and write, but Jonathan insisted that both girls and boys discipline themselves to learn it. The Edwards family even allowed one Mohawk boy to live with them in their house.

Sarah also loved the tribal cultures. She loved the respect the Indian women had for their husbands and their discipline in raising children. They were also very resourceful at making jewelry. As a young girl, Sarah enjoyed luxuries that most of her peers did not. Being the daughter of a well-respected preacher had its benefits and she often went to Boston to purchase fine clothes. She never loved her possessions and was quick to give them to someone in need. When Jonathan came into her life, she almost completely abandoned her taste for luxuries, but it was refreshing to be in Stockbridge where Indians made jewelry and rings for one another.

"We have a special guest today," Sarah said, waving her hand at the door. Jonathan walked into the classroom. "Now, class," Sarah said, pointing at her husband. "Repeat after me, 'Preacher.'"

Jonathan laughed as the kids repeated the word. Since he was preaching that evening, he had already put on his white wig and suit, which was the Puritan tradition that Jonathan strictly abided by. While some preachers in the area had long abandoned that tradition, Jonathan felt proud to stand in continuity with the practices of his ancestors, even if it made him look rather silly.

"Thank you, Mrs. Edwards," Jonathan said with a grin on his face. "Today, I have been asked to tell you a story about Jesus. Does anyone know who Jesus was?"

Several children raised their hands. "He's the Sun," one of them said. "No, he's like a bird because he flew into heaven," another said. Still another child stood to his feet and yelled, "He's the creator of all animals!"

Jonathan remembered his own children's answers to that question. It was a very important question, and many adults he met could not give him the right answer. "Jesus is God," Jonathan said. "But he is also a man." Jonathan paused to listen to the rain trickling down the windows. Claps of thunder shook the wooden house, causing the children to look outside. "And one day Jesus got into a boat and a big storm arose on the sea." A lightning bolt struck in a field, making the whole room bright. The children were growing afraid. "But do you know what Jesus was doing?" he asked.

The children shook their heads.

"He was sleeping like a baby," Jonathan said, lying down on the ground. Jonathan spread out his long body, which had been easier to do in his twenties than in his forties. He could hear the children giggling, but he didn't move a muscle. The storm thrashed against the side of the classroom as the wind made a whistling noise through the shutters. Squinting, Jonathan saw one child approach, about to touch his wig.

"But then he awoke!" Jonathan yelled at the top of his lungs. The children jumped with fear and then laughed hysterically. "And Jesus told the wind to be still and the wind obeyed him. And he told the waves to calm down and they obeyed him too. The sea became as smooth as glass and the boat rocked gently to the safety of the shore."

Jonathan took a bow for his performance as the children clapped their hands. Normally, he would not have entertained his hearers with theatrics, but Jonathan noticed some changes in his teaching and preaching since he moved to Stockbridge. Now, he rarely used notes when he preached and he incorporated many illustrations from nature to help the Indians understand the truths of the Bible. At times, he even waved his hands in the air like George Whitefield to get his point across. He felt relaxed in Stockbridge and his boyish interest in spiders and insects thrived.

Jonathan stood behind the pulpit and looked out at the last of the Mohicans. Alcohol had ravished their culture and these were the remnants of what once had been a great and mighty people. Jonathan had not been in Stockbridge long, but he had come to love these men, women, and children. He saw them not as Mohicans or Mohawks, but as people through whom God would receive glory.

Jonathan looked towards his translator, who was called John Wauwaumpequunnaunt, and nodded for the service to begin. It had taken Jonathan weeks to learn how to pronounce his name, but they quickly became good friends.

"Tonight," Jonathan said. "We will explore the resurrection of Jesus Christ." Jonathan thought about the death of his friend, David Brainerd. He missed him very much and wished David could be there in Stockbridge to help him minister to the Indian tribes. "Everything in the Christian faith depends on the resurrection of Jesus," Jonathan continued. "If Christ had not risen from the grave, we would have no hope to go to heaven. We would have perished in our miserable conditions. But thanks be to God that on the third day Jesus Christ was raised to life. He gave us mercy when we didn't deserve it and grace when we couldn't earn it. And even at this very hour, Christ stands at the door of your heart and knocks. Will you open it to him today?"

Some of the Mohawks stood to their feet and looked behind them at the door of the church. The translator accidentally left the word "heart" out of the sentence and they thought Jesus was trying to get inside the sanctuary. Two of the Mohicans raced to the entrance and pulled the doors open, but Jesus wasn't there. The congregation broke into laughter when John Wauwaumpequunnaunt corrected his mistake.

"You may go through life," Jonathan continued, "pursuing the passions of your flesh. You may numb your mind with alcohol and live an undisciplined life. But none of these desires can compare to the ultimate satisfaction of knowing Christ. To know Jesus as your Savior is beyond any thrill or amusement this world can offer. Make no mistake, the Christian life is not easy. In fact, it's just the opposite. It's extremely difficult. But when Christ wraps you in his arms, there is no other affection like it."

Several Indians stood up and moved around like they normally did during a tribal dance. They were so enraptured by the thought that someone had come to earth to save them that they physically expressed their appreciation to God. "No one has shown kindness to you," Jonathan said. "Not the French or the British. Not even your own neighboring tribes did anything to save you. But Jesus cares. Jesus cares so much that he sent me to tell you about what he has done for you. Men may search for a thousand years to find a treasure as beautiful as salvation, but their searchings would be in vain. Today is the day of salvation. Today is the day of peace."

At the conclusion of the service, twelve Mohicans and three Mohawks gave their lives to God. They were invited to be full members of the church in Stockbridge and Jonathan spoke personally with each one of them, assuring them of their salvation. After the service ended, Jonathan took Sarah and his children outside. The rain had stopped, the wind had blown away, and the sky was scattered with purple and grey clouds.

"I want to be a preacher to the Indians, too, father," Timothy said.

Jonathan looked down at him. "And so you will, my son. And so you will."

Transition Time

Stockbridge, Massachusetts, January 1758 and Princeton, New Jersey, February 16, 1758

"A new position has been offered to me," Jonathan said. "It is time for us to leave the Indians we love."

Sarah lowered the cup of tea she was sipping. "Are you sure this is the Lord's will for us?"

"I am sure," Jonathan replied. "I have spent hours on my hands and knees with God, pouring out my soul to him. This morning I was studying the Scriptures and came across Isaiah 43: 19, 'See, I am doing a new thing! Now it springs up; do you not perceive it? I am making a way in the desert and streams in the wasteland.' God has given me a peace about the things he is going to do through us."

"You always had an uncommon degree of the presence of God," Sarah said. "If this is where God is leading us, I am confident that he will join us for the journey."

"What journey?" Susannah said, overhearing her parents' conversation in the kitchen.

"Your father has been asked to be the president of Princeton University," Sarah said.

Susannah caressed the necklace that her Mohawk friend gave her. "But I don't want to leave," she said. "We've settled here. This is where my friends are. This is where my home is. Why do we have to move?"

"Sometimes God calls us to leave our comfort zones," Jonathan said. "Sometimes he takes us away from home so we can find our ultimate home in him."

Sarah nodded. "And this will also help our family financially. Ever since we left Northampton we have been in a great deal of debt. The Bible teaches us to owe no one anything and by paying off our debt we will be able serve the Lord more faithfully with our resources."

Jonathan glanced out the window and saw Chief Hendrick walking towards his house. Grabbing his overcoat, he went out to meet him.

"It is often hard to submit to God," Sarah told her daughter. "But being a Christian is about giving yourself entirely to his plan. It's about being willing to let God stretch our faith and strengthen our relationship to him."

"But why is it so hard?" Susannah asked.

Sarah walked over to the iron oven and opened it. The smell of fresh bread filled the room. "It's easy to be a Christian when life is easy and we are comfortable. It's easy to submit to his will when we are surrounded by all our friends and family." She took the loaf of bread and placed it on the table. Hot steam oozed out of the cracks in the crust as she sliced a knife through it. "The heat in our lives makes us rise to God. When difficult circumstances pressure us and tempt us, we find that our faith expands and our view of God increases. It is only in the oven of pain and transition that God fully displays his power to us."

Susannah understood that. For her whole life she had watched her father wrestle with the Lord and learn to love him through difficult circumstances. Now it was her turn. "I will pray, mother, that God will make me pliable enough to submit to his will."

Jonathan let out a deep sigh as the cold weather turned his breath to steam. A light snow was in the air, frosting the trees and freezing the river that ran near the village. Jonathan stuck out his hand for Chief Hendrick to shake. "A fine day!" he said, embracing his friend.

"Indeed it is," Chief said, walking next to his friend. Jonathan and Chief Hendrick had known each other for many years. They had benefited from learning about the other's culture and their families had grown close during their stay at Stockbridge.

"I'm leaving soon," Jonathan said.

"I know," Chief replied.

Jonathan looked puzzled. "How did you know? We haven't told anyone yet."

Chief Hendrick stuck out his hand as snow accumulated on his palm. "Isn't it interesting that water from the ocean evaporates, travels hundreds of miles, freezes, and then slowly falls upon our small village here in Massachusetts?"

Jonathan studied this once as a child. "Yes, and they say each snowflake is unique. No two are alike."

Chief Hendrick put his hand in his jacket to warm it. "I knew you were moving because I sensed a change in you. God is preparing you for something else, something different. You are unique, Jonathan. The whole world knows it. There's no one else that has your intellect, your genius. There's no one else that has your passion for holiness. And like the water that travels above the landscape, God is leading you to another city so you may tell them about the One who washes us with his grace."

Jonathan and Chief Hendrick walked down the valley where they often talked about God and his plan for the New World. Ice was forming on the stones near their path and Jonathan was careful to avoid stepping on them. "Princeton is a fine school," he said. "I believe God will make it a pillar for Christian thought. The former president, Aaron Burr, passed away not long ago and they are looking for someone to lead the school in a more God-centered direction."

"You have done great things for us here in Stockbridge," Chief Hendrick said. "You have brought reconciliation to the Mohicans and the Mohawks, not to mention the English residents. Now I want to give you something before you leave." Chief Hendrick reached into his bag and pulled out a tomahawk. "Keep this in your office and may it always remind you that God has already won the victory over Satan."

Jonathan Edwards

Jonathan ran his hand along the sharpened blade. "When I was a boy, my father gave me a tomahawk very similar to this one. I can still remember how happy we were when he came home from battle."

"There's talk of a bigger war, Jonathan," Chief Hendrick said. "It's not a war between our people and yours, it's a war between Great Britain and the colonies. Some even say there's a great revolution brewing in our land."

"That would be interesting," Jonathan said, "if we became a country of our own, completely detached from Europe. If that happens, we should pray that this New World, this new country, would center its formation on God as the Israelites did when they entered the Promised Land."

"We can only pray," Chief Hendrick said. The two men walked a little more until the cold weather had found the weaknesses in their clothes. Chilled to the bone, Jonathan prayed over his friend and took the path that led to his house. "Father God, there's so much work to do in the upcoming months," Jonathan prayed. "Give us strength to sell our house, pack our goods, and travel to Princeton. I praise you for your work here at Stockbridge and ask that your peace will continue to fall upon this town like snow. You have not chosen me to do your will only to abandon me when I need you most. Without your strength I will certainly fall. Without your spirit I will certainly fail. It is you, my Christ, who holds me up when all the world would tear me down. I commit my family and my desires to your care, for I know that your love will not let us go."

Jonathan looked at the crowd. There were young faces and old faces, scholars and students. Each glued their eyes to the new president as they awaited his installation. Jonathan thought back on all the times he had preached in this province. He thought about the awakenings and revivals that took place in years past. He thought about the great men and women who had prayed for him and hosted him in their homes. But most of all, he thought of Sarah, who was still back in Stockbridge moving the house and preparing to travel to Princeton in the Spring.

"As you know," the platform speaker said, "we are deeply grateful for the opportunity to welcome Reverend Jonathan Edwards to our community. Some of you have heard him preach, others have read his books. For those of you who do not know him, allow me to introduce our new president."

Jonathan sat low in his chair. He hated grand introductions. Pride often crept inside him and surfaced on such occasions. "Lord, remind me where I came from," he prayed as the speaker introduced him. "Remind me that without your grace in my life I would be nothing. Without your intervention in my spirit, I would never have chosen or loved you at all."

"Jonathan Edwards has become a household name for us who live in New England. His words have sparked

Jonathan Edwards

awakenings in a land that was spiritually suffering. His book *A Faithful Narrative* describes how God sent revivals to his church in Northampton. His book *Religious Affections* has opened our eyes to how God works through our desires to accomplish his good and perfect will. He has written many other books, essays, and sermons which have contributed to a remarkable outpouring of the Holy Spirit in our land. Please welcome our new president, Jonathan Edwards."

As the crowd stood to their feet and clapped, Jonathan raised his finger to hush the crowd. Too much applause was not appropriate for Jonathan and as he lowered his hand the clapping silenced. He stood tall behind the podium, yet he felt lowly. He felt unworthy to hold such an honored position. He also missed his wife. Few Sundays had passed that Sarah was not in the congregation, looking up at him with eyes that were wide with affection.

"Ladies and gentlemen," Jonathan started, "it is indeed an honor to stand before you this day and humbly accept the position as president of Princeton. I have heard that there are pockets of awakening breaking forth in the student body and I pray that God will continue to show forth his glory upon us."

Jonathan looked across the crowd of people to Nassau Hall, where the classrooms were. Every one of its four stories stood proudly on the campus. Chimneys jutted through the roof into the sky, almost pointing to God himself. The top of the building was crowned with a round white dome that had a directional compass.

"We are living in a time of transition," Jonathan continued. "The old things are passing away and God is raising up new things to take their place. Why, it was not so long ago that I was a college student, studying Greek and Hebrew, preparing for exams, and devoting my mind to the service of God. Some say we are living in a time of enlightenment, a time of science and knowledge. But let us not forget that we will never be truly enlightened until the light of Jesus Christ has burned brightly in our hearts. In times like these we need a compass to direct us." Jonathan pointed at the white dome on top of Nassau Hall. "We need a love for the Holy Scriptures which point us to truth. We need a passion for souls that makes us eager to evangelize our neighbors. And only when we discover the truth found in Christ can we progress into the future."

After the ceremony, Jonathan shook hands with the trustees and some of the students. For many people he was a larger than life figure, not just in height but also in reputation. Many students asked him about George Whitefield, whom they had heard stories of. Everyone wanted to see the man that God had raised up as one of the greatest theologians in their day. Many expected him to be distant and unfriendly, yet when they actually met him face-to-face they were surprised by Jonathan's lowliness and kindness.

"Mr. Edwards, my name is William Shippen," a man said, shaking his hand. "I am a doctor from Philadelphia and I have been asked to inform you and your family about the smallpox disease that is spreading through this area."

"Smallpox?" Jonathan said. "Well, we must be inoculated so we won't contract it."

William grinned. "They said you were a scientist, but I had no idea you knew about inoculations. You are an impressive man, Mr. Edwards. I've never met a preacher before who knew about the latest medical advances."

"Can you tell me about the nature of the disease?" Jonathan asked.

"We do not have much information about it," William said, "but it is killing millions of people in Europe. We think humans contract smallpox by touching someone who has it. When a person is diagnosed with this disease, they break out with small bumps all over their body. A high fever, vomiting, and aching follow. But don't worry, Mr. Edwards, we have lots of faith in our inoculations. By injecting a small dose of smallpox into the body, we can build an immunity against it. In 1721, Lady Mary Wortley Montagu popularized the inoculation for smallpox and while there is no cure for the disease, those who are inoculated won't contract it. I even brought an inoculation kit with me today if you are interested."

"Well," Jonathan said, "I have shaken hands with many people today. Perhaps I should be inoculated immediately." Jonathan led William into the president's house located just beside Nassau Hall. It was much larger than their house in Stockbridge and Jonathan could not wait to show it to Sarah.

As they walked through the white picketed fence, William admired the house. "I've never seen a house with nine windows on the front before," he said. "This is quite presidential."

Jonathan did not care much for human architecture and had not noticed the windows. He preferred God's architecture—the valleys that soak up the rain running off the mountains. "My wife is going to love it," he said, opening the door for him. "She is coming here after she sells the house in Stockbridge. Will you be able to inoculate her and my eleven children?"

"There are plenty of inoculations to go around," William said. "Now I must say that there are many people in Boston and other towns that violently oppose this practice. They say that injecting smallpox into the body is a crime against God and there have even been riots in the streets over the issue."

"As a scientist," Jonathan said, "I can see the benefit of protecting ourselves against this disease. As a theologian, I find no problem with it either. How do we proceed?"

William raised Jonathan's right arm and placed it on a table. "I need you to roll up your sleeve."

Jonathan obeyed.

"Now," William said, lighting a candle, "this is going to hurt, but you must be very still so I can be sure to inoculate you correctly." William reached into his medical bag and pulled out a silver blade. He waved the end of the blade beneath the flame until it was warm and with three even strokes he sliced Jonathan's skin. Blood immediately began to gush from the wounds. "Do not worry, this is entirely normal," he said.

Jonathan squinted. He never liked to look at blood and often grew dizzy when dissecting butterflies and other insects as a child. "If my Savior endured the nails, surely I can endure a simple cut in the arm," he said, feeling the warmth run down his elbow.

William reached into his bag again and pulled out a tube. "In this tube, Jonathan, are the sores from a smallpox victim. I am going to rub them on your wounds to introduce the disease into your bloodstream."

Jonathan shut his eyes and turned his head away as William concluded the inoculation.

"There, that wasn't so bad," William said, wrapping Jonathan's arm in a bandage. "You might experience a very small outbreak of smallpox, but that is normal. Your body will naturally kill the disease."

"Thank you so much," Jonathan said, showing him to the door.

"And if you have any problems, please don't hesitate to send for me."

After closing the door, Jonathan grabbed his arm. It still stung from the cuts, but he knew that in the long run he would be far healthier for having this done.

Jonathan walked into his study and browsed through his books. He trailed his finger along the Puritan classics his mother had taught him. He saw the works of Richard Baxter, John Bunyan, and John Owen. He remembered the struggles of Samuel Rutherford and others who preached the gospel against great opposition. Jonathan sat down in a chair and opened his Bible. His arm stung, but he flipped to Isaiah 53: 5 and read the passage out loud, "But he was pierced for our transgressions, he was crushed for our iniquities; the punishment that brought us peace was upon him, and by his wounds we are healed."

Memories ran through his mind. He remembered the first time he had ever heard that text preached by his father back in East Windsor. He remembered the prayer booth he had constructed to be alone with God. He thought about all the times he had sinned against God, provoking him to wrath, but he had been shown mercy instead. As he thought about his life, a dizziness settled over his head. Perhaps he had lost too much blood in the inoculation, or quite possible he was exhausted from a long day. But he wanted to see Sarah and the children.

"Thank you for bleeding for me," he prayed, stretching out his long legs. "Thank you for loving me enough to give your life for mine. I know I don't deserve it. But you have shown me that you are a God of compassion and forgiveness. Though I am old, continue to give me a fresh faith. Plunge me into the deep and difficult teachings of the Bible and when I come up for air be near to me. You are the Rock of Ages that supports these weary feet. You are the web that I have come to love and lean against."

After removing his shoes, Jonathan curled up in the chair. It wasn't easy for him because he was so tall, but he eventually found a pleasant position and dreamed of brighter things than ever before.

Living Again

Princeton, New Jersey, March 1758

"It seems the inoculation was not a great idea," William Shippen said, examining Jonathan's throat. "Most people who get inoculated experience an outbreak on their skin, but I've never seen a case like this before. The bumps in his throat are preventing him from eating anything."

Jonathan lay on his back, sweating from a fever and starving from lack of food. Every time he took a bite, his body purged it up because of the pain.

"He looks so uncomfortable," Lucy said. "Do you think he will recover from this sickness?"

William placed his hand on Jonathan's swollen neck. "I'm not sure," he said. "If he had contracted the pox anywhere else I would say that he would be fine in a few weeks, but since he cannot eat anything his body lacks the strength to fight off the disease. I'm afraid he's not going to be able to continue teaching his classes this week."

Lucy placed her hand in front of her mouth. "In a way, he spent his whole life preparing to die," she said, clutching her father's hand. "He often talked about death with me and told me not to be afraid. He told me that death is the great entrance to life and I needed to spend my earthly life preparing to live again."

Jonathan, who had been coming in and out of sleep, awoke. "Lucy," he said, "it seems to me to be the will of God that I must shortly leave you. Therefore, give my kindest love to my wife, and tell her that the uncommon union that we shared will last forever. And I hope she will be supported under so great a trial and submit cheerfully to the wonderful will of God. And as for my children, tell them that they will now be left fatherless, which I hope will be a reason for you all to seek the heavenly father who will never leave you or forsake you. And as to my funeral, I would like it to be plain and simple. Any additional sum of money that is given should be immediately donated to charitable uses."

Timothy came in. He had been talking outside the house with the trustees about his father's sickness. "Some of the trustees want to know if father is well enough to preach one last sermon. What do you think, doctor?"

William shook his head. "No, I do not want him to strain his voice. He needs to save his energy."

As Timothy turned to leave, Jonathan opened his eyes. "No," he mumbled. "I will preach to them."

"But you are deathly ill!" Timothy said. "You must stay in bed and recover."

Jonathan mustered his strength and sat up in the bed. "Man shall not live by bread alone," he said, "but by every word that proceeds from the mouth of God. For my whole life I have been fed spiritual food. I have gorged myself on passages in the Bible that told me that all things are possible through Christ. And now, though I cannot eat any more food, the Savior has given me spiritual food to dine upon. I am confident that he will give me the strength to feed the people of Princeton one last spiritual meal."

William was surprised by Jonathan's insistence. "I don't think this is a good idea, but who am I to tell Jonathan Edwards that he cannot preach," he said. "Keep your voice low and don't over exert yourself behind the pulpit. I wouldn't want you to fall."

"I never have raised my voice while preaching," Jonathan said. "Why would I start now?"

William smiled, knowing that some people wished Jonathan showed more enthusiasm behind the pulpit. "I will check on you after your sermon tomorrow," he said. "Now get some rest. You're going to need it."

The next morning, Jonathan's throat burned so badly that he could not even speak. Every time he tried to swallow a sip of water, his body writhed with agony. "God," he prayed, "I know that there is so much in this world I cannot hope to finish. As you know, I want to write my final book, *A History of Redemption*. I want to write about the amazing way you have chosen a people for yourself, brought them out of Egypt and into the Promised Land. I want to write about the early disciples and their love for evangelism, not to mention the reformation of the Christian church. Father, that was my dream, but it appears that you have other plans. Help me to submit to your will, even though I lie here in pain and grief. Help me to know that your ways are better than mine. I don't have to understand your plan, but like Job, I vow to praise you no matter how much my body hurts."

Jonathan rang the bell Lucy gave him by his bed. Whenever he needed anything he always rang this bell and someone would enter the room. "God, before Samson died you blessed him with one last pulse of strength," he prayed. "Samson used it to kill many people, but if you give me one last burst of power, I will use it to preach and save."

Timothy and Lucy helped their father put on his traditional black suit and walked with him to the chapel where he would preach to a gathering of two hundred students. As Jonathan strolled across the grass, his mind flashed back to his boyhood when playing outside in the woods occupied his simple schedule. He remembered the excitement of seeing spiders swinging through the air. He missed those days. He missed the Connecticut River by his house—the quiet sound of flowing water trickling through the grassy marsh. Snakes of all colors swam through those waters—black, orange, red, and yellow. Once, he even caught a green one with his bare hands. He remembered how much faster he could run than his sisters and how his legs often got ahead of his

Jonathan Edwards

body. But now, as he slowly limped across the lawn towards the chapel, his eyes were dim and his steps were slow.

Jonathan entered the sanctuary and walked up to the pulpit. For years he had addressed congregations behind wooden pulpits.

The noisy chapel silenced as Jonathan opened his Bible to Proverbs 9: 10. "The fear of the Lord is the beginning of wisdom," he read, "and knowledge of the Holy One is understanding." Jonathan's voice was weak and scratched, but he strained with all his strength to speak.

"This morning we are going to explore the concept of wisdom and the means by which we attain it. Each one of you has come to Princeton to fill your mind with knowledge and truth. And there is lots of truth to be learned in the world. As a young man, I, too sought after truth. I studied nature and science, astronomy and mathematics. The author of our passage, Solomon, was also a man who sought after truth. He had great wisdom and knowledge."

Jonathan's eyes turned to the front row of boys who were writing down his every word. They knew this might be the last sermon he ever preached. "But all the wisdom of this world will amount to nothing if we do not fear the Lord," he continued. "Oh, there might be a new discovery or a new theory surfacing here and there, but that is not true wisdom. Who knows, my friend Benjamin Franklin claims to be able to harness lightning so we can light our houses in the night. But such achievements do not amount to true wisdom either." The audience whispered at such an amazing idea. "Only those whose souls are saved by Jesus Christ are truly wise," Jonathan said, "and this kind of wisdom comes only from having a relationship with the heavenly father."

After ten minutes, Jonathan knew that he could not talk much longer. His body was too weak to stand. "I must conclude my sermon now," he said. "But I want to tell you one last story. When I was a boy in East Windsor I remember running through the woods with my sisters." Jonathan looked out of the window of the chapel at the piercing, blue sky. "It was a hot summer day," he continued, "and bugs were flying everywhere. And as I ran down the path, I remember seeing a caterpillar hanging from a branch. It had yellow and blue skin and it was twirling in his cocoon. I studied it for several minutes until it disappeared inside its shelter." Jonathan smiled at the memory.

"Never forget, young men, that God uses cocoons to transform us into something better. He uses the difficult times of life, the painful times, the dark times, the war times, to shape us into the image of Christ. You know, Christ understood the darkness. He understood the feeling of loneliness when the great wrath of his father burned against him. Christ was like a spider, suspended over the fire, and God cut the thread of web. He suffered in our place and died in our place. Yet, we are called to die, too. Being a Christian is to die to our sinful passions that separate us from God's fellowship. It's about dying to our pride, our lusts, and our greed. But it's also about living. Even in our moment of death we can be confident that death has been defeated. Jesus Christ was crucified and buried in a tomb, but on the third day he rose again from the grave and ascended to his father in heaven."

Before Jonathan could even conclude his sermon with a prayer, he suddenly collapsed. Timothy, who was sitting next to him on the platform, caught him before he hit his head on the pulpit. The boys in the chapel were still writing down his words as several men carried Jonathan out of the church. His body was long and wiry and dangled as they brought him back to his house and up the creaking staircase to his room. The sores on the inside of his throat had swollen his neck so much that Jonathan could barely breathe. Gasping for air, he lay unconscious and feverish beneath the sheets.

For three more days, Jonathan didn't wake up. When news spread that he was ill, people came from far and wide to visit him and pray over him. Everyone was surprised by his sickness and those who could not visit him wrote long letters to him. When George Whitefield heard of Jonathan's condition, he cancelled his speaking engagements for the whole week and prayed for his friend's health across the ocean.

Sarah, who was also ill in Stockbridge, could not make the trip to see her husband. When she received

America's Genius

news of Jonathan's impending death, she took a piece of paper and wrote a letter to her daughter:

Dear Esther,

What shall I say? A holy and good God has covered us with a dark cloud. Oh that we may kiss the rod of reproof and lay our hands on our mouths! The Lord has done it. He has made me adore his goodness for giving me Jonathan for so long. But my God lives, and he has my heart in his hands. Oh what a legacy my husband, and your father has left. We are all given to God and there we will stay, in the arms of grace.

Sincerely,
Sarah Edwards

The president's house was very quiet on the night of March 22. Jonathan's children had all gone to bed and the only sound was the ticking of the grandfather clock in the dining room. Upstairs, Jonathan's body lay weak and sweating. He was only fifty-five years old, but his life had been a blessing to all around him. He had preached to many people, written many books, and had sparked a spiritual awakening in the New England colonies. The small room where he was sleeping was filled with letters and presents from people he had ministered to. There were even letters from his congregation at Northampton who had removed him from the church. Suddenly, Jonathan felt something tickle his right leg. For the first time in several days, he opened his eyes and looked down at his foot. A small black spider crawled across his body and climbed up the window near his bed.

Jonathan Edwards

"Greetings, Mr. Spider," Jonathan whispered, admiring its shiny body. It was a baby spider, no bigger than his little toe, but in his youth he had seen many of this species and drawn them over a dozen times. The moon was full that night and brightened up the whole room as the spider began spinning a web. Back and forth, up and down. Jonathan traced the spider's movement with his eyes, watching it float to the top of the window and fall to its base. In college, he came to the conclusion that a spider's web was lighter than air and by shooting its spindle into the air, it appeared as though it were flying. By the rate it was going, Jonathan calculated that it would take this spider several days to make its web, but he didn't need to stick around to see it. He knew it would be beautiful and he felt happy that God had once again revealed his beauty to him through nature.

"My work is finished, little spider," he said. "But it looks like yours is just beginning." After taking one last painful breath, Jonathan breathed his last. A smile lingered on his lips as he closed his eyes. The last thing he ever saw was that spider, a creature he had loved and studied his whole life. And with total submission to God's will, he died peacefully in the night.

The next morning, Lucy saw that her father was not breathing. She burst into tears and sent for the doctor who came and pronounced him deceased. Word spread throughout New England that Jonathan Edwards, the great preacher, had died. Most New Englanders had come to know Jonathan through his writings, and the entire region mourned his loss. Princeton held a funeral for him and buried him next to the former presidents.

Samuel Hopkins, a friend of the Edwards family, described Sarah's thoughts: "Though she grieved deeply at her terrible loss, she was quiet and resigned and had those invisible supports which enabled her to trust in God with hope and humble joy." Seven months later Sarah fell terribly ill and died of dysentery. She was buried next to her husband in Princeton. "The way to heaven is ascending," Jonathan once told her, "like a spider's web that is caught in the wind. We must be content to travel as pilgrims uphill, though it is hard and tiresome. But going to heaven is infinitely better than the most pleasant accommodations on earth."

Author's Note

It has been over three hundred years since Jonathan Edwards died yet his memory lives on. His writings continue to spark awakening in the hearts and minds of those who seek to know God intimately and worship him faithfully. Edwards was a powerful thinker in an age of literary and scientific achievement, yet his genius lay, not in his ability to argue the existence of God, but rather in his ability to harmonize God's sovereignty with human endeavor. Edwards had a high view of God's absolute control over reality and he urged his congregations to think clearly about the grace that ordained and sustained their existence. In his own words, "Grace is but glory begun, and glory is but grace perfected."

Jonathan Edwards Timeline

1701	The Collegiate school of Connecticut – later Yale University – is formed.
	Jethro Tull invents the first horse drawn mechanical drill to plant seeds in a row.
1702	William III of Orange dies after falling off his horse.
1703	Jonathan Edwards is born.
	St. Petersburg founded by Peter the Great.
	John Wesley, English evangelist, born.
1705	Isaac Newton knighted by Queen Anne of England.
	The first steam engine built.
1706	Benjamin Franklin, American statesman, born.
1707	The two kingdoms of Scotland and England are united to form the new state of The Kingdom of Great Britain.
1710	Umbrellas become popular in London.
1714	Typewriter invented by Henry Mill.
1716	The first lighthouse in the U.S. was lit in Boston Harbor.
	Jonathan Edwards enters Yale.
1719	*Robinson Crusoe* by Daniel Defoe is published.
1720	Charles Edward Stuart (Bonnie Prince Charlie) is born.
	Jonathan Edwards graduates from Yale.
1721	Smallpox vaccination first administered.
1722	In Russia, Peter the Great ends his tax on men with beards.

1722-23	Jonathan Edwards preaches in New York City.
1724-26	Jonathan Edwards tutors at Yale.
1727	Brazil plants its first coffee. Jonathan Edwards ordained at Northampton Presbyterian church; marries Sarah Pierpont.
1728	Captain James Cook, explorer, born in Scotland.
1733	Religious revival begins in Northampton.
1735	Robert Walpole becomes first British Prime Minister to live at 10 Downing Street.
1739-40	The Great Awakening.
1741	Jonathan Edwards preaches 'Sinners in the hands of an angry God.'
1742	First indoor swimming pool opens in London.
1743	Handel's Oratorio 'Messiah' has its London premiere.
1745	Charles Edward Stuart begins Jacobite rebellion in the U.K.
1746	Charles Edward Stuart defeated at the Battle of Culloden.
1747	David Brainerd visits Jonathan Edwards at Northampton.
1748	Ruins of Pompeii are found. Jonathan Edwards splits from Northampton congregation.
1749	Jonathan Edwards publishes his memorial of David Brainerd.
1751	The first U.S. hospital is founded in Pennsylvania.
1758	Jonathan Edwards offered the presidency of Princeton University. Jonathan Edwards dies.

Thinking Further Topics

Chapter One: Sisters and Spiders

Only God can satisfy the deepest passions of our souls. The Psalmist wrote, "Delight yourself in the Lord and he will give you the desires of your heart" (Psalm 37: 4). What does it mean to delight in the Lord? What are three ways Christians can show God that we love him? Jonathan felt the presence of God by examining God's creation and drawing it in a notebook. You don't have to draw a spider like Jonathan, but find one of God's creatures and draw it in a journal today.

Prayer: "Father, you are the One who sprinkled solar systems throughout the galaxy. We praise you for creating trees, mountains, and oceans. We give you glory for creating birds and spiders. Help us to recognize your greatness through the simple things of life. Amen."

Chapter Two: Swamp Prayers

Jonathan had a quick tongue and a hot temper. Day after day, he asked God to show him how to love people like Jesus loved them. What sins do you struggle with? Pride? Envy? Greed? The Bible says that if we confess our sins to God, "he is faithful and just and will forgive us our sins and purify us from all unrighteousness" (1 John 1:9). Take a piece of paper and list the top two sins you struggle with the most. Find a quiet place to be alone with God like Jonathan, who built a prayer booth in the swamp, and ask Jesus to show you his love, mercy, and grace.

Prayer: "Jesus, we know that you died a terrible death in order to save us. Forgive us for the sins that nailed you to the cross. Create within us clean hearts and fresh attitudes. Give us minds that think only about you and hearts that beat with your love. Amen."

Chapter Three: Food Fight

Sometimes it's difficult to do the right thing. Jonathan saw his friend, Elisha, throwing food in the cafeteria and when the teacher asked who was responsible Jonathan did the right thing and told the truth. Think about the times when it was hard for you to tell the truth. Does telling the truth make you popular? The Bible says that God has "showed you, O man, what is good. And what does the Lord require of you? To act justly and to love mercy and to walk humbly with your God" (Micah 6: 8). It's never easy to act justly, especially when our friends could get in trouble. But it is far better to please God than to please people.

Prayer: "Give us courage, oh God, to do the right thing even when everyone around us doesn't. You say in your Word that you require us to walk humbly with you, but we confess that our pride gets in the way. Protect us from ourselves. Shield us from our own selfishness. And give us strength to love you despite our weaknesses. Amen."

Chapter Four: Dock Discipline

God created the body to be disciplined. We discipline ourselves by studying, praying, reading, and working. The author of Hebrews wrote: "No discipline seems pleasant at the time, but painful. Later on, however, it produces a harvest of righteousness and peace for those who have been trained by it" (Hebrews 12: 11). Jonathan struggled to discipline himself. He kept a diary of his weaknesses in hopes of discovering disciplines that would draw him closer to Christ. Write down your weaknesses and match a spiritual discipline to each. For example, if you struggle with gossip, practice the discipline of silence. If you struggle with jealousy, meditate on Bible verses that deal with being content. Before long, if you are faithful with your disciplines, you will see improvements and your life will look more like Jesus.

Prayer: "Father, we look to you for guidance on how to control our sinful appetites. Thank you for giving us disciplines like prayer, fasting, and meditation that point us beyond ourselves. We praise you for demonstrating perfect discipline through Jesus Christ who came to earth and submitted to your holy will. Take from us what we do not surrender and continue to conform us into the image of our Lord."

Chapter Five: Cured by Sickness

When was the last time you got really sick? Perhaps it was the flu or a stomach virus. Remember how terrible you felt? Even though life is painful, God has given us pain to protect us. If we couldn't feel pain, we would hurt our bodies without knowing it. God also uses pain to draw us into his presence. The Psalmist declared, "Before I was afflicted I went astray, but now I obey your word" (Psalm 119: 67). Jonathan often fell sick. He suffered from fever, exhaustion, and eventually smallpox. But Jonathan understood that it is only in the darkest moments, the painful and sorrowful moments, that he saw Jesus the brightest. How has pain pointed you to God?

Prayer: "Jesus, we confess to you today our struggles with pain and suffering. We confess our inabilities to handle hardship the way you handled it—without sin. Teach us to trust you even in the difficult times. For we know that you go before us, behind us, and beside us on this journey of life. Amen."

Chapter Six: Judgment Day

The Bible is God's Word given to us to teach us about Jesus and show us salvation. But it also has great advice about how to live. Proverbs 1: 7 says, "The fear of the Lord is the beginning of knowledge," and Mark 12: 31 says, "Love your neighbor as yourself." By obeying truths like these we are shaped into the image of Jesus

Christ. What's your favorite Bible verse? Think about how best to apply it to your life today.

Prayer: "God, we praise you for communicating yourself to us through the Holy Scripture. You have shown us how to correctly think, act, live, and love. Each day is a blessing from you and we ask that you give us a deeper passion for reading the Bible. Give us a greater understanding of its truth. And help us share the good news of the gospel with everyone we meet. Amen."

Chapter Seven: Awakening

Going to church should be our favorite activity of the week. The Psalmist declares, "Worship the Lord with gladness; come before him with joyful songs" (Psalm 100: 2). Jonathan loved going to church. He loved watching people come to know Jesus through sermons and songs. Yet, even when he wasn't in church he still worshipped God. Every stroll through the woods, every carriage ride across the pasture, he saw God's glory on display and he entered the presence of God. How are you worshipping God outside of church?

Prayer: "Lord, send an awakening on our hearts. Show us more of yourself that we might love you more and serve you better. Guide us in your truth as we worship you throughout the course of every day. We praise you for Sunday, our day of rest, and we ask that your Holy

Spirit make our hearts throb for you, both now and forevermore. Amen."

Chapter Eight: Last of the Mohicans

When was the last time you shared Jesus with someone? Before ascending into heaven, Jesus told his disciples, "Go into all the world and preach the good news to all creation" (Mark 16: 15). Sometimes it's not easy to tell someone about the love of God. It can feel awkward and scary. But God promises to be with us. He promises to give us his Holy Spirit. Jesus said, "But you will receive power when the Holy Spirit comes on you; and you will be my witnesses in Jerusalem, and in all Judea and Samaria, and to the ends of the earth" (Acts 1: 8). Jonathan loved to tell people about Jesus. When his church kicked him out, Jonathan preached to the Mohawk Indians because he knew that God wanted them to hear the gospel, too. Find one person today to share the gospel with. It might be a friend, a neighbor, or a family member. Pray that God will give you strength as you are obedient to the Great Commission calling on your life.

Prayer: "Jesus, you tell us that you will give us the power of the Holy Spirit as we proclaim the light of your truth in a dark and dying world. Fill us with bravery as we uplift your name to those who have never heard it. Surround us with your power as we share your love with the lost. And continue to assist us as we become your hands and feet in a world that is not our home. Amen."

Chapter Nine: Transition Time

How do we know what God's will is for our lives? Jonathan had a big decision to make. A position opened up at Princeton to be the president and he didn't know what to do. Paul wrote: "Do not conform any longer to the pattern of this world, but be transformed by the renewing of your mind. Then you will be able to test and approve what God's will is—his good, pleasing and perfect will" (Romans 12: 2). Every one of us makes decisions every day. Pick one of those decisions and pray about it. Ask God to show you his will and always remember that God informs us to transform us.

Prayer: "Lord, we come before you today eagerly admitting that we have trouble making big decisions. Teach us to have faith in your control over this world. You tell us in your word that your will is perfect and pleasing to you. Thank you for including us in your divine activity and adopting us as sons and daughters of a heavenly home. You are the Great Teacher and we, your students, commit to listen more attentively to your words as we obey your commands. Amen."

Chapter Ten: Living Again

Are you homesick for your heavenly home? God has promised us a greater and more abundant life after this one. Jesus told his disciples, "In my Father's house are many rooms; if it were not so, I would have told you. I am going there to prepare a place for you. And if I go and prepare a place for you, I will come back and take you to be with me that you also may be where I am" (John 14: 2–3). Christians should live as though they will one day live again. We should view life like Jonathan did—with eyes upward. Near the end of his life, Jonathan was ready to meet his Savior face to face. Have you ever wondered what heaven will be like? Paul wrote, "Our citizenship is in heaven. And we eagerly await a Savior from there, the Lord Jesus Christ" (Philippians 3: 20). Are you living a life that eagerly awaits the Savior? How would such a life affect your friendships, decisions, and prayer life? Write down your thoughts and prayers in a journal. Keep your thoughts fixed on God and he will direct your steps.

Prayer: "Oh God, Father, Son, and Holy Spirit, you are the Creator and Governor of the universe. You are Judge of all. We thank you for your mercy. We praise you for your loving kindness. Detach us from our pride and restore us when we stray from your Word. Teach us to walk lightly on this earth, knowing that there is another life to come. Show us fresh grace every day. Continue to remind us that you have prepared a place for us in heaven where we will gaze at you forever. We pray this in the name of our Lord and Savior, Jesus Christ. Amen."

Life Summary

Jonathan Edwards was born in America in 1703 and died in 1758. He was a preacher, teacher, writer, and university president who loved nature, mathematics, and science. His life goal was to exalt God by telling people about his glory and lead them to a saving relationship with Jesus Christ.

Jonathan attended Yale University when he was thirteen years old, became a preacher in New York and Connecticut, and became influential in the revivals that were occurring throughout New England. After leaving his church in Northampton, Connecticut, Jonathan moved to Stockbridge where he ministered to the Mohawk Indians. He then was invited to be the president of Princeton University where he died of a smallpox inoculation shortly after his arrival.

Through his life, Jonathan Edwards wrote sixteen books and hundreds of sermons and articles. He is best known for his sermon, "Sinners in the Hands of an Angry God" and his book, *Religious Affections*. His biography of David Brainerd, a missionary to the Indians, made him widely famous. In his lifetime and today, Jonathan Edwards is recognized as an American genius, philosopher, and theologian who sparked great revival in the hearts and lives of those who wanted to know about God's love, mercy, and grace.

Quotes of Jonathan Edwards

Quotes or paraphrases of Edwards in this Trailblazer Book:

Page 45: "I will continue to lift you up every day, for you are highly exalted and powerful. Your glory has become the object of my eyes and I will forever praise your name."

Page 54: "The Lord has not brought me this far," he said, "only to abandon me when I need him."

Pages 55-56: "God does not punish his people," Jonathan said. "Sometimes he chooses to discipline them and refine their character, but it was Jesus Christ who paid the ultimate punishment for our sins. It was Christ who stood before an angry God and took the punishment in our place. It was Christ and Christ alone who satisfied the wrath that our sins provoked. And so, when we find ourselves struggling with temptations, let us remember that either we will discipline ourselves or God will. If you truly are a Christian this morning, I encourage you to discipline yourselves before Almighty God. Pray harder, fast longer, and train your spirits to be sensitive to the voice of God."

Page 57: "Like the Old Testament Israelites who were led into the Promised Land, God has brought our ancestors to the New World. But when we stray from his covenant, when we grow lazy in our faith, judgment will come to us like it came to those Israelites who forgot that 'he who ignores discipline despises himself, but whoever heeds correction gains understanding.' So let us give ourselves completely to God, both in action and in attitude. And may we thank our Father for disciplining his children instead of punishing us."

Page 67: "I feel like a new man. The fear of dying awakened heavenly appetites within me and I once again seek to serve God with all my heart. I believe God has just cured me with sickness."

Page 72: "There are some of us," he continued, "who care little for our souls. We come to church every week, but curse Christ to his face by showing no respect for God by participating in idle chatter and foolish talk during the sermon."

Page 73: "Guard well your souls this day," Edwards continued. "For we are not promised another. Trust in Jesus and depend on his grace and God will save you from an eternity without him."

Page 75: "Great movement always generates great friction," he said. "We should not run away from difficult situations, even earthquakes, because whenever God is at work in this world building his kingdom and saving his people, Satan is there too, trying to tear down our faith."

Pages 86-87: "Not long ago," Jonathan said, "Whitefield wrote me a letter in which he told me that Benjamin Franklin had asked him if they wanted to go to Ohio and start a colony that would be a better example of Christianity to the Indians than what we have here in Connecticut."

Pages 89-90: "My text this morning is Deuteronomy 32:35," he said, "'Their foot shall slip in due time.' "Your wickedness makes you heavier than lead," Jonathan said with a soft voice. The people strained their ears to hear him. "And your weight bears down upon you, pulling you in the very bowels of hell." "All your righteousness cannot save you any more than a spider's web can stop a rock that is passing though its spindle." "The wrath of God is like a rising water, swirling and increasing in intensity. The bow of God's anger is bent against you because of your sin and the arrow is ready on the string and nothing but the mere pleasure of God keeps the blade from being drunk with your blood." "The God who holds you over the pit of hell, much as one holds a spider over the fire, is dreadfully provoked by you. He is so pure and holy and you are so vile and loathsome, yet his strong and unwavering hand does not let you go. He is angry with you, and there is no reason to keep you safe, but he wraps you in his fingers so that you will not fall away. Oh sinner! Consider the fearful danger you are in." "God can save each and every one of you today," Jonathan concluded his message. "But never forget that he will give you his mercy, not because you deserve it, but because you need it."

Page 100: "I believe God will save many souls in this town," Jonathan said, looking at it over the Housatonic River. "It is a prototype for future missions where people of different backgrounds and traditions live in harmony. In fact, it is the very picture of heaven."

Page 107: "You may go through life," Jonathan continued, "pursuing the passions of your flesh. You may numb your mind with alcohol and live an undisciplined life. But none of these desires can compare to the ultimate satisfaction of knowing Christ. To know Jesus as your Savior is beyond any thrill or amusement this world can offer. Make no mistake, the Christian life is not easy. In fact, it's just the opposite. It's extremely difficult. But when Christ wraps you in his arms, there is no other affection like it."

Page 115: "Ladies and gentlemen," Jonathan started, "It is indeed an honor to stand before you this day and humbly accept the position as president of Princeton. I have heard that there are pockets of awakening breaking forth in the student body and I pray that God will continue to show forth his glory upon us."

Pages 125-126: "God," he prayed, "I know that there is so much in this world I cannot hope to finish. As you know, I want to write my final book, *A History of Redemption*. I want to write about the amazing way you have chosen a people for yourself, brought them out of Egypt and into the Promised Land. I want to write about the early disciples and their love for evangelism, not to mention the reformation of the Christian church. Father, that was my dream, but it appears that you have other plans. Help me to submit to your will, even though I lie here in pain and grief."

Page 132: "The way to heaven is ascending," Jonathan once told her. "Like a spider's web that is caught in the wind. We must be content to travel as pilgrims uphill, though it is hard and tiresome. But going to heaven is infinitely better than the most pleasant accommodations on earth."

Some Further Jonathan Edwards Quotes

"Prayer is as natural an expression of faith as breathing is of life."

"Resolution One: I will live for God. Resolution Two: If no one else does, I still will."

"Grace is but glory begun, and glory is but grace perfected."

"The happiness of the creature consists in rejoicing in God, by which also God is magnified and exalted."

"Sincere friendship towards God, in all who believe him to be properly an intelligent, willing being, does most apparently, directly, and strongly incline to prayer; and it no less disposes the heart strongly to desire to have our infinitely glorious and gracious Friend expressing his mind to us by his word, that we may know it."

"True liberty consists only in the power of doing what we ought to will, and in not being constrained to do what we ought not to will."

"To pretend to describe the excellence, the greatness or duration of the happiness of heaven by the most artful composition of words would be but to darken and cloud it; to talk of raptures and ecstasies, joy and singing, is but to set forth very low."

"As God delights in his own beauty, he must necessarily delight in the creature's holiness which is a conformity to and participation of it, as truly as (the) brightness of a jewel, held in the sun's beams, is a participation or derivation of the sun."

"There are two sorts of hypocrites: one that are deceived with their outward morality and external religion; many of whom are professed Arminians, in the doctrine of justification: and the other are those that are deceived with false discoveries and elevations; who often cry down works, and men's own righteousness, and talk much of free grace; but at the same time make a righteousness of their discoveries and of their humiliation, and exalt themselves to heaven with them."

"Can the believing husband in Heaven be happy with his unbelieving wife in Hell? Can the believing father in Heaven be happy with his unbelieving children in Hell? Can the loving wife in Heaven be happy with her unbelieving husband in Hell?"

"I assert that nothing ever comes to pass without a cause."

"If I get a jump right, there's a feeling of flying."

Sources and Bibliography

Primary source: Marsden, George. *Jonathan Edwards: A Life*. Yale University Press, 2004.

Secondary sources: Various Edwards books and sermons including *Religious Affections* and *Resolutions*.

Tertiary source: http://edwards.yale.edu/

Jonathan Edwards' Works

Resolutions (1722-1723)
These writings were Edward's guidelines on how to live in total dependency on Christ. Most of these resolutions were written when Edwards took his New York pastorate and subsequent stay in East Windsor.

Distinguishing Marks (1741)
This work was originally delivered as a commencement address in regards to the revival controversies that were breaking out in New England. While he did not persuade his audience at Yale, his words were published in Boston and later in London.

A Humble Inquiry (1749)
Edwards wrote this book to explain his decision to change the requirements for entering full communion. This book was a reaction against nominal Christians who did not take their faith seriously when it came to church membership.

The End for which God Created the World (1765)
This book was written in response to philosophers in Edwards's day who argued that human happiness was the greatest of pursuits. Against these claims, Edwards

contended that God's glory was the greatest of ends and Christians must live in recognition of this.

Religious Affections (1746)
Perhaps his most influential work, Edwards argued for emotional and intellectual balance in the life of the Christian. He explained that God gives us affections so we can know and love him more.

The Nature of True Virtue (1765)
Edwards suggested in this dissertation that there are different levels of virtue, the best being union with God. Known for its ethical dimension, *The Nature of True Virtue* stands as one of the best ethical works of the day.

Personal Narrative (c.1740)
In this book, Edwards reflected on his religious experiences and spiritual insights as a pastor. Pulling from his diary entrees, he communicated the means through which God brought him into holiness and gives valuable insight into God's saving grace and the human need of forgiveness from sin.

Life of David Brainerd (1749)
Inspired by the life of missionary David Brainerd, Edwards read through Brainerd's diaries and wrote a biography about him that was to become a wide spread work of literature that brought instant recognition. Since Brainerd died in his home, Edwards developed a strong friendship with him and tells his story in a winsome way.

Freedom of the Will (1754)
One of his most timeless works, Edwards confronts the prevailing notion that the will is unaffected by human depravity and therefore can make decisions with great

neutrally. In *Freedom of the Will*, Edwards exalts the sovereignty of God and suggested that people act either towards sin or holiness.

Faithful Narrative (1737)
In 1734-35, reports of revival breaking out around Northampton grew and Edwards provides a detailed account of these spiritual events. Written from the standpoint of an observer, Edwards's work became a model for those who oversaw the spreading of revivals.

Original Sin (1758)
Against the accepted view that human nature is essentially good, Edwards wrote *Original Sin* to uplift the doctrine of human depravity. Edwards suggested that only after the brokenness that comes through a realization of sin do humans accept the grace that God gives to the sinner.

Sinners in the Hands of an Angry God (1741)
This sermon is what Edwards has become so famous for. Originally preached to the congregation of Enfield, Massachusetts, it began to be printed in textbooks throughout New England. Throughout the sermon, his theology of God as the holy and righteous judge and man's need of grace emerged.

Justification by Faith Alone (1738)
Written against the widespread belief of Anglican Arminian theology, Edwards carefully examined the doctrine of Justification and relied heavily on his Puritan fathers for spiritual insight. This complex discourse of material includes over ten years of work and thought.

History of the Work of Redemption (1739/74)
After the death of Jonathan Edwards, some thirty sermons

were recovered and published in Scotland. In this masterpiece, Edwards unpacked the history of redemption on a cosmic scale, revealing God's plan of salvation that was constructed from the beginning of time.

Humble Attempt (1748)
Through a correspondence with revivalists in Scotland, Edwards wrote this book to uphold the primacy of prayer as it relates to the work of God. In this work, he discussed scriptural proof for prayer and included crucial statements about the future of the church.

Some Thoughts Concerning Revival (1743)
Throughout New England in the 1740s, spiritual revivals swept the landscape. Many opposed these revivals because they were viewed as irrational behavior, but Edwards defended them as mighty acts of God. He cautioned those who opposed the work of God and instructed them not to damage the outbreak of Christian zeal.

OTHER BOOKS IN THE TRAILBLAZER SERIES

Augustine, The Truth Seeker
ISBN 978-1-78191-296-6

Paul Brand, The Shoes that Love Made
ISBN 978-1-84550-630-8

John Calvin, After Darkness Light
ISBN 978-1-78191-550-9

Amy Carmichael, Rescuer by Night
ISBN 978-1-85792-946-1

Fanny Crosby, The Blind Girl's Song
ISBN 978-1-78191-163-1

Billy Graham, Just Get Up Out Of Your Seat
ISBN 978-1-84550-095-5

John Knox, The Sharpened Sword
ISBN 978-1-78191-057-3

Eric Liddell, Finish the Race
ISBN 978-1-84550-590-5

Robert Moffat, Africa's Brave Heart
ISBN 978-1-84550-715-2

D.L. Moody, One Devoted Man
ISBN 978-1-78191-676-6

Mary of Orange, At the Mercy of Kings
ISBN 978-1-84550-818-0

Patrick of Ireland: The Boy who Forgave
ISBN: 978-1-78191-677-3

John Stott, The Humble Leader
ISBN 978-1-84550-787-9

Christian Focus Publications publishes books for adults and children under its four main imprints: Christian Focus, CF4K, Mentor and Christian Heritage. Our books reflect our conviction that God's Word is reliable and Jesus is the way to know him, and live for ever with him.

Our children's publication list includes a Sunday School curriculum that covers pre-school to early teens, and puzzle and activity books. We also publish personal and family devotional titles, biographies and inspirational stories that children will love.

If you are looking for quality Bible teaching for children then we have an excellent range of Bible stories and age-specific theological books.

From pre-school board books to teenage apologetics, we have it covered!

Find us at our web page:
www.christianfocus.com

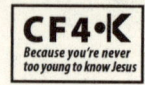